Meeting The Prophet In My Reflection

Ken Cox

Copyright © 2021 by **Ken Cox**

All rights reserved. No part of this publication may be reproduced, distributed or transmitted in any form or by any means, including photocopying, recording, or other electronic or mechanical methods, without the prior written permission of the publisher, except in the case of brief quotations embodied in critical reviews and certain other noncommercial uses permitted by copyright law. For permission requests, write to the publisher, addressed "Attention: Permissions Coordinator," at the address below.

Ken Cox/Rejoice Essential Publishing

PO BOX 512

Effingham, SC 29541

www.republishing.org

Unless otherwise indicated, scripture is taken from the King James Version.'

Meeting The Prophet In My Reflection/Ken Cox

ISBN-13: 978-1-952312-92-2

LCCN: 2021918281

TABLE OF CONTENTS

INTRODUCTION..1

CHAPTER 1:   The Prophet and Seeing Reflections..3

CHAPTER 2:   The East Wind Prophet..........................11

CHAPTER 3:   The West Wind Prophet.........................18

CHAPTER 4:   The South Wind Prophet........................25

CHAPTER 5:   The North Wind Prophet.......................35

CHAPTER 6:   The A/Q of a Prophet.............................44

CHAPTER 7:   The Now Generation: Lost Faith in the Prophet...52

CHAPTER 8:   The Communication of The Prophets Perception...............................61

CHAPTER 9:   The Prophet, Generationally Blessed and Weak at the Same Time..................68

CHAPTER 10 :   How God Sees the Prophet on Another Level...75

CHAPTER 11:   Prophets Moving in The John the
                Baptist Anointing....................................85

ABOUT THE AUTHOR..93

Introduction

I WAS INTENSELY MOVED RECENTLY in a whole new way. I already knew that everything I had encountered, suffered, and experienced has been for the glory of God, according to Romans 8:28. My zeal to learn and know more about the prophetic moved me to the revelations I will share in this book.

I hope that you, like I, used the pandemic to learn more things about God. I did and, in turn, learned more about myself also. The image of what I saw reflected what I was fighting to understand within me. The image of my mentality drove me to where God revealed.

My assignment is to share with you about meeting the prophet within yourself, your gift and the process of connecting your personhood to its specific gifting. We must first become the best version of ourselves.

You find the keys to understanding yourself in what you are seeing and experiencing. We see the reflection of life and the life we live, from the inside to the outside. Witness a revelation of life that you need to realize. Meeting the prophet you are now and this person will become your reflection.

Grow as a person, and you will grow as a prophet. This process is essential to your growth and connecting with your gift. Let us now start the discussion of who you see when you see a reflection of yourself. Let us meet the prophet that is within you. Say it with me, "I'm meeting the prophet in my reflection."

CHAPTER 1

The Prophet And Seeing Reflections.

*A*NYONE ELSE OUTSIDE OF me ever wondered about the way in which Scripture describes the basket we see Moses in as a small child? How did the basket float and not sink? Was it mud, was it tar? But whatever it was, we know that the basket did not drop or fall because what God had inside was important.

What was inside the basket was important then, as it is today it is still valid. The keyword here is inside. Let me explain, as we start with the one God has called to a nation.

We are talking about Moses, God's prophet. He is said to be the greatest, if not clearly one of the greatest of all time. The reality of reflections is what we see in the life of Moses.

There is one Scripture that changes the life of Moses forever. Exodus 2:12-14 reveals a reflection of what was on the inside of Moses. Let us determine the definition of a reflection. A reflection is the image of something in a mirror or on any

Meeting The Prophet In My Reflection

reflective surface. In the case of Moses and other prophets, we can look at a reflection as the inside mirror reflecting on the exterior part of our lives.

Here is Moses, a Hebrew, raised as an Egyptian. His status was that of a prince. He had the finest clothes, and he was highly educated. He ate the best foods of his time, and he had his pick of any woman he desired.

Moses was part of the culture of the cutting-edge technology of his time. Whatever was happening in the Egyptian empire at that time, rest assured that Moses was a part of it. What is funny is that it took adversity to reveal the opportunity of his lifetime.

Moses was to be the heir to the throne. Let us look at the fact that he is brought up as the grandson of the Pharaoh. Time and man's placement put him in this position. He was groomed for the position, but something within him was wrong.

Would he accept the fact that he is a new type of Egyptian and ignore it? Or would he be true to his heritage and pursue a struggle to connect with it? The fact was that Moses was a Hebrew; yet the struggle of self-reflection was wearing on him.

Let's fast forward; Moses was in his 40's. He just entered the next phase of his life and was blessed beyond measure. He had everything, and yet he had issues.

The Prophet And Seeing Reflections.

Imagine Moses, blessed with everything, but there was an element of confusion within his life. Can you relate to being blessed and still confused with trouble on the inside of you? You are walking around, and you are trying to figure out who you are? Moses was a Hebrew, raised as an Egyptian; yet there was a part of him that knew he was not an Egyptian. He was stuck in a place of having no identity.

The prophet who can see reflections of themselves can relate to Moses here as he sees himself or herself as Moses did. He is on the cutting edge, but he knew he did not belong because he was different. Does this describe you?

Moses was a troubled human being struggling with the basic instincts that demand that to belong somewhere. We all strive to have a place, a group, or somewhere that we know we belong. All Moses had was bottled-up reflections of who he was and where he really belonged. Can you relate?

Now look at Exodus 2:12-14, and now you will see what Moses saw. He saw two men fighting; one was a Hebrew and the other an Egyptian. To Moses, this was more than two men fighting, it reflected what was going on in him, and now he saw it with his natural eyes.

Moses was seeing a reflection of what was truly going on in his life. He saw it on the outside. So many times, the things we see in life reflect what we experience on the inside. Our outside mimics what is occurring on the inside of us.

Meeting The Prophet In My Reflection

There is drama on the outside because there is drama on the inside. Are you a prophet who always speaks about the trouble that follows your life? Maybe you need to check your love walk. What is on the inside will show up on the outside.

Have you ever known a gossiping prophet? They have the gift to look in your face, smile, and then talk about your business or anyone's business that they may speculate about. Sit down with that prophet, and you will find that they have issues making real friends and building real relationships. That's the reflection.

Understanding what you see and experience on the outside reflects what you have on the inside. Would Moses accept the fact that he is a new type of Egyptian and ignore it, or would he be true to his heritage and pursue a struggle to connect with it, the fact that he is a Hebrew? This is a truth he had to accept.

Prophet, take inventory of your life right now. What do you see when you look and how long has your "it" been there? Moses saw the fight between these two men as a fight within himself.

He has dealt with the personal struggle for 40 years. Moses confronted himself as he interfered with their fight. Moses now had to make a choice in his life after 40 years. So many of us as today's generation prophets are reluctant to make important life choices of this magnitude. When we do, we still have trouble following through on the plan and process of God for our life.

The Prophet And Seeing Reflections.

Moses chooses his heritage, and yet he, like so many of us, is still troubled. The problem is that he is clearly still in a position of an identity crisis. He made a choice in killing the Egyptian.

He is still at the palace, but he finds out that he has no platform with the Hebrews or the Egyptians. Exodus 2:12-14 proved that, as the next day, Moses saw two Hebrews fighting, and he was frightened as his conversation with them exposed him the future prince, as a murder of Egyptians.

Moses positioned himself as a leader for the Hebrews, but he was not their leader yet. People knew Moses as he is referred to as a prince and even a judge by his own Hebrew brethren. Of course, word spread in one day of his exploits with the two Hebrews.

The two Hebrews tell him of that, but in reality, he is in an impossible situation. Imagine the inner reflections of Moses upon hearing this. His Hebrew brethren speak prophetically upon his life, and he did not realize it. He heard the rumblings of the people about what happened, and the reflections of his torment produced fear.

Maybe you are a prophet who, like Moses, is tormented on this inside, and you're on the verge of greatness. But before you can deal with the greatness connected to your life, you must deal with the reflection of what's not going on in your life.

Meeting The Prophet In My Reflection

We now see Moses going through a phase of displacement. Displacement is the place where God moves you from the current place, to where you're thinking is beyond the present place.

Moses found himself in frustration, hopelessness, fear, and at a table full of newly experienced emotion. Moses did not realize that his displacement caused by his sin was how God was getting him ready to lead the children of Israel out of bondage.

Moses was able to experience 40 years of reflections on what his people had felt for 400 years. The reflections of the 40 years were the picture of the leader to whom Moses was to become. Mentally he was becoming a leader.

Moses, the Egyptian Hebrew, went into the wilderness dealing with the reflections of being in a place where he was an outsider. Yet, everything he saw was something that God had placed in his life for him to be able to consider the magnitude of who he was to God.

Can you imagine Moses is in the wilderness with a 'Prophet to the Nation' mentality? Even with that, the reality is that he was still growing mentally.

The lesson we learn is that we are not ready to lead for God until we are ready mentally. We may be gifted with all the gifts, but it is God who will show you the reflections of your life as he is dealing with you.

The Prophet And Seeing Reflections.

When you understand the reflections of your life, you will understand the vision God has for your life. This should entice you to learn needed lessons for the mission ahead. Moses learned a valuable lesson in his life. When a Prophet of God can understand the reflections of his or her lives, then they become able to grow in their gifting in an accelerated place.

Today's prophet is wise to understand that they may be anointed but will have to wait to be appointed; Moses waited 40 years, David waited, Joseph waited, Elisha waited as well as many others.

The prophetic gift will constantly be tested. While you are gifted, you will not be able to escape the tests of your mantle. Just as God showed Moses, God can show you; let us look at the reflections that as God is showing you.

We all have reflections if we will only look at them and communicate with God on the issues of our lives. This is a lesson that every Prophet of God learns in his or her special way.

Exodus 2:12-14 changed Moses, or was it merely a reflection of what was on the inside of Moses. In this chapter, we've identified a reflection as an image of something in a mirror or on any reflective surface. In the case of Moses and other prophets, we can look at reflections as the inside mirror reflecting onto the outside.

Meeting The Prophet In My Reflection

When you understand the reflections of your life, you will understand the vision God has for your life. This entices you to learn needed lessons for the mission ahead. '

Let us now deeply examine and understand the reflection of our lives. Moving forward to the next four chapters, we discuss the 4 Winds and what the reflections of these winds mean to us, and how you and I will connect with those reflections. Prophet, let us now discover more about ourselves.

CHAPTER 2

The Ministry of The East Wind Prophet

LET'S SEE IF YOU see a reflection of yourself in The East wind Prophet. Elijah and John the Baptist were East wind prophets. As we look at the Hebrew word for wind is ruah, which is a symbolic meaning of "spirit." The word, in both Hebrew as well as Greek, is translated as "spirit." The wind represents the Holy Spirit of God. This is the same Holy Spirit mentioned on the day of Pentecost, when the Holy Spirit fell upon men. Act 2 says that they were filled.

The mindset and mentality of the wind blowing in the East wind direction is a metaphor for the sun itself to rise in the east and set in the west.

The wind is a biblical element of the truths found in Psalm 78:39 and Jeremiah 22:22. The "four winds" is a phrase used principally to describe the whole of the earth or heaven, encompassing all directions or the "four corners" of the earth: north, south, east, and west (Jeremiah 49:36; Matthew 24:31).

Meeting The Prophet In My Reflection

No prophet can be delivered, changed, and transformed apart from the work of God's winds! In this chapter, I want to explore if you have an East wind reflection of yourself. This would equate to you being an East wind prophet.

Change is the keyword here for the East wind. The East wind represents both blessing and cursing. "The angel is ascending from the east in Revelation 7:2 with the seal of God along with multiple angels coming from the east as a vehicle of change. Remember, the East represents change and renewal of status, like from evil to good.

Revelation chapter 7 is filled with east wind references that are set to change evil to good. Are you the prophet who always sees evil, and everybody else thinks things are okay? This is the essence of the East wind and its assignment.

There are many definitions we can assign to the East wind. The most important thing we realize about an East wind is it rebukes evil. You see yourself as that standard of God among your circles. There is a level of maturity here that an East wind Prophet realizes about themselves.

It is a judgmental wind, Genesis 41:27 and 1 Kings 18:21. This wind is destructive and confrontational. 1 Kings 17:1 is the reflection as there are prophets that God calls like the East wind. There are certain things that happen when an Eastern prophetic wind blows.

The Ministry of The East Wind Prophet

There are certain things that happen when an East wind prophet enters an area. God will use these prophets, and The East wind, like Elijah and John the Baptist, were East wind prophets. Today, we should all want the John the Baptist anointing in this new generation, and I will discuss it later.

The wicked Israelites would tell you today that God used natural disasters to destroy them because of their disobedience to Him. In Israel, winds typically blow from the Mediterranean Sea inland in an eastward direction. This brings cool, moist air and rain during the winter months.

The east wind can be deadly as it blows across the desert. The desert east wind was well known to the prophets as a dry wind from the ground. The east wind dries up fruit like a wind of fire. This is a consuming fire that often prophets spoke of in their prophetic visions. Can you see your reflection here as an East wind prophet?

Let us not forget Hosea. In Hosea 13:15, Hosea speaks to the idolatry and sinfulness of the people of Israel that the suddenness of his word would come from an east wind. This is how the manifestation of his word would occur. This wind would be a sudden wind that would cover the entire Land of Israel. There will be a total drying up of all water.

The East wind is a blast of wind from God that dries up resources; this is God's wind of destruction. The goal of the east wind is to destroy evil. As you look for yourself here, my question is, do you ever wonder why people may shun you, even though you know you have God's gift upon your life? Think for a minute, and you may see the revelation of your destiny and why everybody cannot walk with you.

The prophet Ezekiel 19:10-12 Ezekiel shares about the destruction of the Kingdom of Judah at the hands of Babylon by an east wind: Again, the East wind dried it up. Ezekiel refers to the "east wind" as "fire."

Isaiah 32:1-2 Isaiah describes the realities of the East wind in visions that are all drawn from natural realities like rocks, streams, wind, and rainstorms. The destructive wind he describes is a wind of change. It's an East wind.

Then there is Job 27: 19-23. He describes the east wind and the effects of it changing and drying up everything around it. Job, who many do not see as a prophet, but his life mirrors the prophetic guidelines of one of God's chosen servants.

Job talks about this as he shares the cruelness of life. He is the poster child of having and then not having. Change is a trait of the East wind prophet. This is how God deals with you; can you relate to this.

So many times, you think it is punishment, and it is the will of God bringing you to another place in him. Job is human, and he compares God's punishments to the sudden terrifying power of a windstorm. He says that "The east wind lifts them, and they are gone; it sweeps them out of their place."

David in Psalms 55: 6-8 is in one of the absolute worst times of his life. David wants to fly away from the evils of the present and find shelter in the wilderness in his time. Can you see how he compares his life to the difficult circumstances he is undergoing to a windstorm and tempest?

The prophets who know God understand that the phenomena of the East wind are not just for the Land of Israel. An East wind Prophet should be able to see the "east wind" in effect even today. As we see that God parted the Red Sea, the East wind blew on the sea and caused Israel to walk over dry land? This is a specific type of change from evil to good. Can you see your reflection in this type of wind?

The East wind is the wind God uses in times of trouble. This is a day of trouble we live in. Is the East wind Prophetic Anointing critical to Prophets today? In Eph 5:6 -16 and Col 2:8, we are warned not to be deceived by "vain words" of the "sons of disobedience." Our discernment must identify these types of prophets and people. Their reflections and interactions with others must expose them.

James 2: 20 especially speaks about the rich Laodiceans, who have misjudged the poor. Today we see this spirit in prophets and people who talk faith but have no works. They bind burdens on others, but they would not carry them. Today as Matthew 23:4 points out that they teach the world to keep commands and to love their neighbors, but they fail to do so. This prophet will use God's name in vain in their lives, but they will not practice what they preach or obey God.

Meeting The Prophet In My Reflection

Ex 20:7 speaks about the rich men, when they speak "vain" things, without works, bring punishment on themselves, and again the east wind fills their stomachs. They get discipline from them.

Today, if you are an East wind prophet, you must be careful. We have so many prophets who profess visions constantly, but our lives do not align with God's vision as we say. Cleary we see 'vain" visions?... Ezekiel 13:7 says the "prophets" of Israel are "foxes" because they have seen "vain visions."

They see 'vain' visions because God does not reveal things to them anymore. So, they see and speak vain things. They were "not" building the way God wants them then, and the reality is some of us are guilty of this now. Isaiah 66:12 God will send them a "stormy wind" and an "overflowing shower." The Gentiles are the overflowing shower.

When King Solomon sinned by "going after other gods," God called him an 'evil' man (1 Kings 11: 5- 11). As the punishment, God said that He would take the Kingdom and give it to his 'servant.' The same will happen now as the prophets in Jerusalem have seen vain visions.

The East wind Prophet, the Lord's anointed, must be worthy to follow in this day and time. But Jesus also taught an essential truth about the servants He sends to us in the new generation. "He that receiveth you," He said, "receiveth me, and he that receiveth me receiveth him that sent me." The most important role of an East wind prophet is to teach us of the Savior and lead us to Him.

The East wind Prophet is the ultimate Watchman on the tower, protecting us from spiritual dangers we may not see or we choose to ignore. The great Ezekiel got a word from God as he said, "You are my watchman, and what I tell you to speak, you will speak.

We live on a planet clamoring with a million voices. The internet, our smartphones, our bloated boxes of entertainment all plead for our attention and thrust their influence upon us, hoping we will buy their products and adopt their standards.

The prophet's voice, while spoken kindly, will often be a voice asking us to change, to repent, and to return to the Lord. When correction is needed, let's not delay.

And do not be alarmed when the prophet's warning voice counters popular opinions of the day. As you are humble in following the counsel of the Lord's prophet, I promise you an added blessing of safety and peace.

You and I have sampled, The East wind prophet; let's move to the West wind prophet. Not all of you will see your reflection here with the East Wind prophet.

You may see parts of yourself, but not enough to claim it as your mantle or introduce yourself like that. So, let's look at the West wind prophet. Let's look for your reflection there!

CHAPTER 3

The Ministry of The West Wind Prophet

LET US CONTINUE AS now we seek to understand our reflection as a West wind prophet. Of all the winds that must blow upon the earth, none are like the West wind. The West wind is the wind of restoration.

The West wind brings the wisdom of God, astute counsel to release His plans, purpose, and strategies. To know the heavenly plans and to apply them practically upon the earth. The West wind is always contrary to unbelief. When the West wind blows, God will always restore.

Exodus 10:15-19 speaks of Moses' reflection of the locust's destruction upon Egypt and the deliverance and restoration upon Egypt with a strong west wind. We see the locusts, and cast them in the Red Sea. Moses is both a West wind and North wind Prophet, as I will share later.

The locust is a representation of demonic spirits that the East wind removes. We can also say that The West wind is a deliverance wind also. The West wind deals with deliverance from demonic spirits, and Prophets who walk in this calling also deal with deliverance and restoration from demonic Spirits. Let us be real: walking in the true deliverance gift requires great sacrifice.

Keep in mind that the East wind deals with the devil's works, evil itself, while the West wind deals with demons themselves. It's a wind that brings the person a total deliverance from curses. We could say that David was an example of a man that was a West wind prophet. Can you see any area of your life that will connect you here as a West wind prophet?

The qualities of David are many as he is primarily a warrior and king. I constantly choose to group David with Samuel, a prophet and a judge, and the entire prophetic community of that day. I, like many others, also called David a prophet of God.

David led a complex life. One of his most lasting contributions was the numerous prophecies he wrote down for our learning and to give us hope (Romans 15:4). Please also understand that the Apostle Paul indicated he considered David one of the greatest of the Old Testament prophets.

God used David mightily as a prophet and prophetic scribe to introduce many of God's promises in his writings, the Psalms. David says, "The Spirit of the Lord spoke by me, and His word was on my tongue." In David's prophetic work of Psalm 22, we see a specific and detailed description of Christ's crucifixion that has at least nine prophetic references to the suffering of Jesus Christ.

I want you to look and find yourself here, especially prophetic scribes who God divinely inspired to write about his plans and purposes as you share a divine revelation. Let me ask you again, do you see yourself as a West wind prophet? Does your reflection reflect this about you?

The level of David's prophetic gift does not seem to get a lot of credit. David's prophetic gift is seen in the description of Christ's last hours: Psalms 22, where we see David write the following: "My God, My God, this is what Jesus said, "why have You forsaken Me, where have we seen this at?" Matthew and Mark attest, Jesus Himself spoke these words as He was about to die. How prophetic is this? Are you a David-type West wind prophet?

Look at David; he is a prophet and in relationship with God who had sworn with an oath, now destroys his enemies as a man of war. He was able to conquer all the enemies of Israel. This is the same David, who would play for Saul, such that the demonic spirit upon Saul would depart from him (1 Samuel 16:23).

Soon after David was king, we see the incident of the wind in the tops of the Mulberry Trees (I Chronicles 14:14-15). The Philistines felt they could unseat David, and they battled back and forth. David had been victorious, yet we see the Philistines keep coming back to try once again.

David inquires again of God. God tells David not to go after them but to turn away from them and come upon them over against the mulberry trees. God tells David of the wind sound in the tops of the mulberry trees.

This will be the sign that God has gone out before them. They were delivered before the battle started. Notice that God was specific on what he wanted David to do. David had clear, direct orders where to go and what the wind would do. You want the wind of the Lord to blow in our lives? We need to understand the West wind directives from God.

The West wind prophet will come to know, depend on and understand this. This is your reflection for some of you; this is where you know that you are a West wind prophet.

Your reflection as a West wind prophet will bring you a sureness of who you are because of your relationship with God. Let look at the facts that David knew:
1. Knew God's voice.
2. He did not have to be baited to listen for His voice.
3. He was obedient to His voice.

David here demonstrates precision in his dealings with God. This is a West wind prophet knowing God and being comfortable in his or her execution of the assignment.

The great Prophetess Deborah was also a West wind Prophetess. Judges 4:4 offers that Deborah, a prophetess, the wife of

Meeting The Prophet In My Reflection

Lapidoth, judged Israel at that time. She set the Israelites from bondage. Deborah was a mother in Israel, anointed by God.

While Israel chose new gods; then there was war. Deborah brought a message that freed the people from curses and ushered them to the wind of liberation and restoration, the West wind.

The West wind prophet is a Seer of trends like Prophetess Deborah. What is God showing you right now about what he will bring restoration in a specific area of your life or others? We will be wise to realize that we are always in need to be the first partakers of God's purposes.

In Mark 6:45-51, there came a time when Jesus had to deal with the wind in His disciples' lives as well as dealing with the wind in the lives of Prophets and the people of God today. The Word says that the wind was contrary to them.

Just like the disciples trying to get to where they wanted to go rather than where God wanted them to go. Many prophets today who feel they are walking in the Spirit find the wind of the Lord is contrary to them.

This type of prophet will claim the anointing and the ministry of the West wind Prophet, but their life is constantly at odds with God; they are always looking for miracles, and there are none. This type of prophet will continue to be passed by because of unbelief. Let us consider the fact if that is the reflection that life is showing you?

Every prophet needs to understand that when the wind is contrary, the Lord is attempting to change our direction to walk with Him. Prophets, when we change directions, instead of the West wind in your face, it will be at your back, and it will push you in directions that God wants you to go.

The West wind Prophet must be one of extraordinary faith. This only comes with a relationship. Look at David's and Deborah's lives as a reference. Today, when God gives a prophet an assignment, his peers or others may not always see it or understand. There can be much talk, gossip, and slander attached to that prophet's name. Some of you have seen this in your lives or the life of others.

Think about this: if the disciples had known the Word of God, they would not have been surprised. If the prophets of today and God's covenant people knew his Word, we would not be jealous of others and digging ditches to destroy our peers.

The West wind prophet must understand that the work of God is only when the older man is destroyed, with his old nature and his old way of thinking, that we will be born of the Spirit. Therefore, we hit and miss today in the prophetic. That is not acceptable.

The West wind Prophet will know God and know that God will work miracles, signs, and wonders. The West wind prophet, born of the Spirit, becomes like the wind because they are part of the wind.

Meeting The Prophet In My Reflection

God moves by His Spirit; this is how The West wind prophet operates also. Prophet, some peers will not know where you're coming from, nor should they be expected to. Do not worry about that. There will be empowerment time.

Joel 2:7-11 "They shall run like mighty men; they shall climb the wall like men of war; and they shall march. Joel, a West wind prophet, spoke of the 'Day of the Lord,' or the 'Day of God's judgment'. With judgment comes the restoration.

So now we have looked at the East wind prophet, and this chapter has been dedicated to the West wind prophet. My objective is for you, my prophetic reader, to open yourself up and find yourself. Let us remember that we have gathered ourselves here to see the reflection of what is going on in our lives. We are just like Moses.

When we become better people, we'll become better prophets and seers. If you have not connected with either the East or West wind prophets, let's see if you connect with the South wind prophet. You have never seen wind like a south wind. Get ready; let's see now.

CHAPTER 4

The Ministry of The South Wind Prophet

YOU MAY SEE YOURSELF carrying others and simultaneously operating under challenging circumstances with all the pressure from others.

To further complicate matters, let us look at some facts about believers. Most believers don't believe God sends judgment upon people or nations since He is a loving God.

Most people only see one aspect of God's nature, the God of love. They don't believe He will judge because they don't believe God will follow through on his promises. This is why a prophet's job can be difficult and sometimes frustrating. The reflection of difficulty you see is accurate. You are a South wind prophet.

Non-believers mock the thought of God and usually blame Him for all the bad in the world. Interesting? On the one hand, they do not believe He exists, and on the other hand, they blame him for the evil done to the innocent.

Meeting The Prophet In My Reflection

Prophet, you must understand as a South Wind Prophet, you will also deal with this personally. People will call you a false prophet or say that prophets do not exist now and then want to come to you for prayer or a word from God. The reflection of difficulty you see is very real. You are expected to know how to handle it.

Humans cannot give life to themselves. Only God is the creator of Life, and only He has determined that all humanity must die once and face judgment. The South wind is a force of God that will exercise judgment. Some of you will see this reflected in your life as you will be seen as a prophet of judgment.

Tornadoes, hurricanes and other tropical storms ride on the South wind. What makes the South wind so unique? These are divine miraculous winds that the South winds carry that God uses to reverse the enemy's curse and release many of us from the enemy's traps.

These winds are our arm of faith to access "Divine Grace" to function on our behalf for the purposes started with Abraham. Notice in Genesis 20:7, the King has him scared and planned to sleep with Abraham's wife. God told the King in a dream, do not proceed.

God restores him from this oppression and frees Abraham to do great works such as to be a blessing to the King to spare his life as God would accept the prayer of His prophet. This is the mark of a South wind prophet.

When the children of Israel were in bondage in Egypt, they were not just delivered; there was a restoration that took place through the promise of God to Abraham.

A South wind is therefore a restoration wind. Job 37 says he talks about the heat of the sound wind and the quietness of the South wind. South wind restores that which has been stolen or destroyed by the enemies.

We all have had friends like Job. They finished their critiques of Job as most people will when they feel down. We then see the Spirit-filled young man, Elihu, began to point out the things in Job's life that were displeasing before God, and he uses the South wind in his description (Job 37:17).

Elihu points out the connection between the East and South wind, and we see it throughout Scripture. Job is a classic example of someone who has endured. The South wind prophet is always able to endure and prepare. Can you remember how God brought you out of some of your mess despite you and your efforts?

The South wind is the wind of Divine Grace. As we study the South wind, the South Wind Prophet must be aware of who they really are and what they do for mankind. Your call as a South wind Prophet requires much in your life. Many times, you are going to be the sacrifice that God will use for the demonstrating of his purposes. Some of you are feeling this as you read this chapter.

Meeting The Prophet In My Reflection

The South wind blows, and it brings a confident quietness to the people of God. We need to note that when the Spirit of a man is quiet before God, that allows his servants to hear from God. Luke 12:55 says, as we see a south wind blowing, speak and it will come to pass. Some will say this is prophesying with the wind.

The South wind is the God ordained spirit, which identifies people prepared to inherit the promises. Some even call it a "deliverance" wind, unlike the West wind or the East wind. The South wind is always associated with the concept of "drawing out" and "setting apart."

The South wind will rescue, recover, and cause to escape enemy oppressions by a body of delegated and empowered people to the freedom to worship God in Spirit and truth. When you see these traits in your life as you reflect these things, you are undoubtedly a South wind Prophet. You are the prophet of rescue; you are always there for others.

We also see this south wind mentioned in the book of Songs of Solomon 4:16. It says, "and come, thou South; blow upon my garden, that the spices thereof may flow out." This is a promotional wind that is pleasant, and yet it is also the most dangerous.

Additionally, in Acts 27:13, Paul journeys toward Rome, it says: "When the South was blowing softly, things were well, everyone felt safe, and we see that the order was given to set sail." The ship set sail, and the south wind changed.

The wind was soft, the South wind ceased to blow, and a mighty Northeast wind came down from the mountains. The South wind has been blowing gently in their lives, and those aboard Paul's ship were enjoying their complacency.

We also see that there were 14 days and nights when neither Sun nor stars could be seen. What happened? The South wind changed, and now we see another side of it.

The sailors had lost all hope of being saved. Finally, there was a sea wreck on the rocky cliffs right off the island of Malta. It was the treacherous South wind.

The wind changed. The South wind has tempted them out of the safe harbor, and now it has opened them to tests. This is a testing wind, and you must trust God in the trial of temptation. Therefore, South wind Prophets always seem to be tested repeatedly.

Every prophet will have to deal with temptation, but especially the South wind prophets. The enemy wants to keep you off your assignment because most South wind prophets are multi-gifted.

Prophet, how many times in our life have we prayed to God to be delivered. Temptation is one of the many things that will face South wind prophets. We often pray with one eye open, looking at the very temptation we are praying to be delivered from. In other words, the South wind Prophet finds themselves in a series of tests constantly.

The necessity of the Prophet's ability to deal with temptations and other distractions from God can be summed up in three things. These three things are traits of a mature prophet and the foundation of a South Wind Prophet.

1. The Sin of a person or prophet will always begin with a simple phrase, "As we think, it is in our heart." Prophets, you can "Sow a thought, reap an act. Prophet, you can sow an act, reap a habit. Prophet, you can also sow a habit, reap a character; sow a character, reap a destiny!" The question is, what will you do?

2. Secondly, you must want deliverance. Whatever it is that is not in your best interest, physically, mentally, and in all areas of your life, let it go. This is a testing wind, and you must trust God in the test of temptation.

This is why South wind Prophets always seem like they are being repeatedly tested spiritually. Your will must be devoted 100%. This is not even debatable. The wrong attitude can destroy you, and without question, will lead to defeat (1st Corinthians 10:13).

3. Something better must take the place of that which is harmful in your life. It does not matter if you are fearful; you

must successfully get rid of the negative by replacement with something positive and more fulfilling.

Many of our now generation prophets are captured by fear, lust, jealousies, anger, and no doubt a multitude of tormenting adversaries. The Issachar Anointed prophet was excellent because this type of prophet was willing to abandon their very soul for God.

Their will yielded to the will of God. This is why the enemy wants you tempted and unfocused. By now, I hope you have seen the complex battle that many times a South wind prophet will engage in.

Luke 4:18-19 supports the Spirit of the Lord is upon Me, as I minister to those who are poor, some captive, some blind, but in all cases, they need something. They need something they do not have. This is the theme of a South wind prophet.

Once as prophets, we are delivered from the traps of Satan; now, we are free to soar in the Spirit to receive additional wisdom and revelation essential for our maturity and growth.

For prophets, the release of His grace will begin to set free those in prison and captivity from the oppressions and snares of this world. The reality is the enemy has imprisoned the body of Christ but now is a time of deliverance, like we have never seen before.

Meeting The Prophet In My Reflection

God restores through the anointing of a South wind prophet. Daniel was also a South wind prophet. In Daniel 9:2, the prophet would labor for seventy years in the desolations of Jerusalem. He interceded for the restoration of Israel.

The South wind is a prosperity wind. Daniel was in high positions in the land of Babylon. Daniel was preferred above his peers because of his excellent Spirit (Daniel 6:3). We all should strive in our gifts for the excellence of anointing that Daniel possessed. His gift was extraordinary.

Luke 15 details one of my favorite prosperity stories, as we see a young man, better known as the prodigal son returning because everything has gone wrong in his life.

A deeper look at this Scripture shows a young man who went from owner to employee. The very essence of the South wind has come to deliver us today from this type of oppression, especially economic oppression in all forms.

God has called us as his servants to be CEOs of the work He has given us. The South wind births the promises of God in the lives of his prophets. Look at Abraham; he was a South wind prophet of God. He was rich in cattle, silver, and gold. God says in Genesis 12:2 that He would bless Abraham.

Abraham's life presents us with the lessons of a South wind Prophet. Notice in Genesis 20:7, the king has him planned to sleep with his wife. God told the King in a dream not to do that.

God restores him from this oppression and frees Abraham to do great works such as to be a blessing to the King to spare his life as God would accept the prayer of His prophet. This is the mark of a South wind prophet.

The very essence of the South wind has come to deliver us today from all types of oppression, especially economic oppression in all forms. God has called us as his servants to be CEO of the work He has given us.

You are looking at your reflection. Do you see yourself as a South wind prophet that God has called us as his servants to be CEO of the work he has given us?

The south wind births the promises of God in the lives of his prophets. South wind prophet, perform your duties and assignment with honor. You are in the company of Abraham, Daniel, and others, to say a few.

Study the examples of prophets in specific winds. We all grow more robust and more effective as we learn more about the reflections we see in our lives. The South wind has a special godly connection with the East Wind, as it sets the pace for the South wind to be ushered in.

The South wind will bring and will equip the prophet with the peace of God. The South wind will also bring whatever is needed for understanding. Some of you will identify with me in the next chapter as we discuss the North wind Prophet and the reflections we see as North wind prophets are so unique.

Meeting The Prophet In My Reflection

The Psalmist Asaph wrote: "He, meaning God, has caused an east wind to blow and now by his actions, we have God as he has brought in the south wind"(Psalm 78:26). We see the same message in Philippians 4:7. Make it your mission to get to know yourself better as a South wind prophet. Those of you who see your reflection here know you are blessed.

Remember this, the prophet that does not know who they are is lost. They are ineffective due to lack of a reference point.

CHAPTER 5

The Ministry of The North Wind Prophet

THE WORD OF GOD reveals the mysteries of the four winds. In the previous three chapters, I have shared with you the four winds, all except the North wind.

There is no wind like the North wind, and as unique as the others are, the North wind is unique within itself. I find myself a North wind prophet, yet I see my reflection in the other winds. Still, I settle within myself as a North wind prophet.

We all know that God determines when and which of the four winds will blow upon mankind. Therefore, note that a North wind is a wind that originates in the North and has special significance. This wind signals cold weather and seasonal change in the Northern hemisphere. It is surprising to learn that the north wind is hot in the Southern Hemisphere, leading to bushfires. At the same time, there are many attachments to the North wind, which will also bring God's fire. So, we do refer to it as a Fire of God through the wind.

Meeting The Prophet In My Reflection

The North wind is the release of the 'Prosperity of Grace', opening the door for a reserved provision that the people of God will be the beneficiaries and participants in God's end-time plan. Song of Solomon 4:16 says, "Awake, O North wind. Awake!" There is a position of honor as we experience the North wind.

To understand the North wind, we first must realize that the origin of the North wind comes directly from the throne of God. This symbolizes power, majesty, and authority, while the South wind is symbolic of comfort, refreshment, quietness, and temptation.

The East wind brings judgment that deals with the source of evil. The West wind blows as the sun sets and reveals the end of the day.

The North wind Prophet stands and symbolizes the tree of the righteousness of God. The restoration of all things, as it deals with the demons of evil. Song of Solomon 6:11 says, "We are the nuts and the fruit of the seed of the trees." As North wind Prophets, it is us; we are His trees of righteousness.

The North wind prophet will see God constantly checking the fruit we have produced in our lives; therefore, we may be seen as trees. Think of the North wind prophet as the enforcer of the prophetic standard.

The North wind Prophet is a driven mission originated; this prophet sees things other prophets may simply ignore. This type of prophet is significant on protocol, as it reflects being a standard-bearer of God. As you look at yourself and your calling, do you see a reflection of yourself here?

As a North wind prophet, we see the North wind blow upon us so that the spices may flow out of our lives. As the anointing rests upon us, spices are the sweet-smelling fragrances and the healing balms of God. Can God use you in this manner?

The Apostle Paul spoke in II Corinthians 2:15 he says, "we are a sweet savor of Christ." The North wind blows upon God's prophets and his people; they will partake of the fruits of the Spirit. Proverbs 25:23 shows us that the North wind can bring the presence of God in the rain, and it can take it away also.

When we experience a North wind, we experience the release of grace. The door of spiritual provision is available. God's grace and favor set apart a people to be the beneficiaries and participants in the Father's great end-time plan. God has special plans for his people.

In Ecclesiastes 1:6, Solomon declared about the North Wind: "The wind goes toward the South and turns about unto the North." The North wind, according to Solomon, continually brings God's deliverance and refreshment constantly in the earth.

God has made the North wind always available to us; only we have not come into a place to receive it. Prophet, can you understand that despite your mantel, you still have room to grow. Can you see this in your reflection?

The North wind is categorized by several different images, such that we see in the life of the prophet Joel. Joel 2:23 says God hath given you the former rain, which means revival.

God will use his servants to bring revival to the land. The North wind carries the image and Spirit of revival. The word rain is synonymous with revival filled with the presence of God. Are you a prophet sent to the nations to conduct revivals and to bring people to Christ?

1 Samuel 12:18 says that God sent thunder and rain, and the people greatly feared the LORD in the presence of Samuel. Here the North wind is bringing transition, which means a change. This wind is opening new chapters and closing other branches. Samuel was a North wind Prophet.

When Samuel came, the era of Judges transitioned from to the age of Kings. Samuel's life represented a time of change for judges as they were no more, and we see that kingship started. North wind prophets need to understand that you will have an abundance of friends or close associates. Your key is to recognize your covenant partners sent by God.

North wind prophets must realize that your life and ministry represent a significant change. The reason is simply that this type of prophet will never accept the status quo and will always

The Ministry of The North Wind Prophet

stand for the changes that God is employing in a region or a nation. This is fundamental for a Prophet called to the Nations.

Samuel offers up a burnt offering, as the Philistines came near to attack Israel (1 Samuel 7:10). God used the thunder with a great voice, and the Philistines were confused and defeated before Israel. Transition as victory is closed for one nation and open for another country.

1 Samuel 3:21 - God reveals himself to Samuel. The ministry of Samuel as the ministry of a North wind prophet will manifest the presence of God.

This book has mentioned Moses in a variety of winds, but you must admit he is also a North wind Prophet. His life and ministry came to the scene, and God brought a transition that took place in the lives of the children of Israel.

Exodus 34:29 is another classic tale of transition as we see Moses came on mount Sinai with the Ten Commandments. The color of his skin, face, and face shone while he talked with him. This represented change again. The presence of God will change you.

Read Amos 7:14-15. Amos is a North wind prophet. He is a herdsman from Tekoa. He declared that he prophesied not out of personal choice. He says that God took him from following the flock and inducted him into the prophetic ministry. Here we see the transition for a whole new lineage of prophets. He is an outsider who God has called to the front line.

Meeting The Prophet In My Reflection

Look at Hosea 1-3. The question is: can you handle a life of public shame and embarrassment as a prophet for God? Does your title mean more to you than the shame you may inherit? Look at Hosea's life of public shame. As a prophet married to a prostitute, Hosea reflects a significant change as God took his life and mimicked the situation with Israel. Oh, the life of a North wind prophet.

All these prophets represent a common trait: North wind prophets are very conscious of God's summoning and sustaining them as they seek to reveal his message to the people. They were obedient in whatever manner he chose to use them.

The North wind prophet will consistently demonstrate growth into the "conscious experience" of the soul's confrontation. Today we see The North wind prophet grow stronger and stronger in their conviction as they mature more and more.

The North wind prophet is a prophet marked by the living God with a mantle that "is central and determinative." The North wind prophets of today find inspiration in the accounts of how they were led into the prophetic ministry.

The North wind Prophet of the Biblical days and today is constantly under the lengthened shadow of this initial experience with God. It affected the totality of their ministries and life relationships. You will always identify a North wind prophet as they will exhibit a deep, inward, personal experience with God.

The Ministry of The North Wind Prophet

The North wind prophets like the South wind prophet, East and West wind prophets were inducted into the prophetic ministry with inspiration and revelation.

Sometimes the North wind prophet must realize that God allows the North wind to blow harshly upon us. Then there are other times it blows just enough to help us take the next step. Every prophet who has a North wind mantle should realize this.

Understanding this is the same principle for the church and body of Christ today. The North wind blows upon us, and we get exposed. We start to see just how non-vital we are, that we are not building up the Body of Christ, we are not living for Christ at home/at work/in the church life.

This is when we should thank God for his mercy & grace. God does not leave us as we are, but He blows the North wind upon us to bring us on, even though we do not deserve it.

This North wind is referred to as a "blowing wind" in our situation. Often, the North wind prophet will holler about the intense life storm they are going through.

We still do not realize that God is the master director of our life, as he uses this wind and the anointing it brings to prepare us for more fantastic experiences. The Spirit of God will visit us to stay with us as an overshadowing cloud.

Therefore, many North wind prophets will never be exposed even in our most vital moments as the Holy Spirit reveals only

Meeting The Prophet In My Reflection

what God will use to bring Himself glory. At the same time, he will take care of our needs.

Thank God for His gracious visitation of the excellent North Wind, known in some circles as the "blowing wind." Can you see your reflection as a North wind prophet?

The North wind will enhance our personal and corporate experience of God! Blow upon us and show us our real situation/condition, and then help us enjoy and benefit to a maximum of your overshadowing as the visiting-to-stay cloud! There is a true statement for all North Wind prophets.

Just as North wind prophets have launched upon their prophetic careers by a definite call based on relationship, Israel did the same thing. Because of a covenant relationship with God.

Therefore, every prophet should study all the winds to see some traits of your life in different winds, and your mantle will be enlightened and your anointing will increase to do greater works in your assigned calling. The North wind prophet must constantly be sensitive to God, no matter what physical or emotional trials are going on around us. Prophet, allow this door to open your soul. You will reflect the qualities of a North wind prophet.

We must be willing to allow God in our life as he blows the North wind. The good seasons remind us of the very promises of God. The hard seasons awaken us to the requirements for our upcoming lessons in life. Welcome to the ministry of the North wind prophet.

We have covered the four basic types of prophets; we all should fit in somewhere. Some of us are multiple fits. All that is good but now do we have the A/Q in our prophetic DNA to move forth in God. Do you see this in your reflection? Moses did not until he saw trouble and had to make a choice.

What is the A/Q of a prophet? It is which type of adaptable quality? We will now discuss dealing with your life and being able to function and define the A/Q of a prophet.

CHAPTER 6

The A/Q of every Prophet

As a prophet, Seer, watchman, or even an Apostle, take note of your life quickly and think about some things you have seen and the things that have become standards in your life. If all you have ever seen is poverty, poverty is all you will know, even with wealth. If all you have seen is sickness, then all you will ever know is sickness, and you will literally be sick. What is your reflection showing you about yourself?

The idea of being happy in life may escape you because you may have been exposed to drama, failure, and evil, and that is what is attracted to you in life because you are more familiar with those experiences. If the truth is spoken, most of us will not want this in our lives, but we will accept it because it is normal. Then know your "Adaptable Quality" (A/Q) is low.

This is a term usually associated with business operations. The term Adaptable Quality is also easily applied to every prophet. The reality is that every leader needs to have an adaptable quality, especially the prophets of God. God will put us in situations that we will need to be the element of change.

Before we can be effective, we will need to understand that we will need to be changed and developed ourselves. Some of you, as you read this, are seeing your reflection as just this.

Some of you will struggle to understand why a prophet needs an A/Q. Keep growing, my prophetic friend; trust the fact that God does have plans for your life.

All others, for the prophet, an adaptive quality dramatically increases performance without compromising who you are in God. God can trust you more in the performance of your duties or assignments to his calling upon your life.

The now-generation prophet has an identity issue as we struggle to gain the trust and confidence of God's people. The people of God have a right to know that their prophet is open to growth, which opens the prophet's adaptive quality.

The prophet must display the ability to act upon what God has called them to do. Fair or unfair, the people of God need the skills and equipping of the prophet to be on point. The prophet or seer is the solution provider that's in touch with God and has the transfer needed for the people of God.

Look at Acts 3:2. The story of a man, lame at birth, and he had to be laid at the city's gate daily. All the man's life, he was lame. This was his normal; this was all he could do. This was all he could look forward to because of his situation. He had to be laid there daily, so he depended upon someone to do that for him. His sense of independence could not have been developed because it was not normal for him to walk independently.

He was a man, and his view on life had to be tainted because his normal was not what we would call normal. His normal was what many of us describe as dysfunctional. He is like many of us, as our normal is only normal because we accept it as normal. In reality, our normal is dysfunction just like the lame man. When you look at your reflection is this what you see?

Developing a leader, especially a prophet, is a process that takes the individual through change, moving out of their comfort zone. The person moves into a process that challenges the individual to the core of who they are in order to develop who they will become.

Welcome to understanding the A/Q of the prophet. This is the adaptable quality that so many of us avoid developing because it so changes us in the process. We do not like to change.

Prophet, has the normal in your life become less than enough? Think about that. Has the normal in your life avoided the process of the A/Q in your life because you felt it was ok to be angry, sad, depressed, bitter, moody, or wishy-washy? You thought it was ok because it was your normal.

Have you ever forgotten what day it was because all you do is a daily routine? The reality of a new day is lost in your life;

the reality of a recent morning means absolutely nothing. This morning is like the rest because you find yourself ending up in the same position every day, doing the same thing every day.

In Acts 3 again, we look at the lame man at the gate. The zeal of life within him is not burning because he is constantly begging for alms. How many prophets are sitting today, tonight, in places that are seemingly dead to them because every day in their life is the same, all the time? Nothing changes because you never realize that you can change.

Maybe God has sent someone into your life, and you rejected the changes they brought because you knew the changes were disruptive to your normal.

The lame man at the gate simply expects alms. He does not expect to heal. Notice that this man is having his life called to a different normal.

He must do something different for a change and more specifically for healing. Oftentimes, we will not do this because it challenges our ability to exercise our adaptable quality.

Why would you leave what you are accustomed to? Why leave it when you are comfortable with it. Now the lame man looks at something differently and challenges his Adaptable Quality of life. You have seen his conflict. Is it relevant to yours? Do you expect to be healed like he was, or have you given up because it does not seem appropriate? What is the reflection of yourself showing you?

Meeting The Prophet In My Reflection

The Scripture says he gave heed unto them, expecting to receive something of them. The expectation for him went to a whole new level. His feet and ankle bones received something they never had strength. He began leaping, shouting, and he even entered with them into the temple, walking, leaping, and praising God.

You must now think about what was going on inside of his head. Did he ever believe that he could be healed? What had he heard of God that would make him praise God for his healing? Whatever it was had been hidden inside of him and not reflected for his purposes of trying to live.

Let's review: Moses had a similar mental adjustment as he witnessed the two men fighting. He had to make a choice, just as the lame man did. He made a quality decision based on his life and knowing there was more. Moses also had that issue inside, that reflected a need for a new life in Christ on the outside.

The lame man is the metaphor for the Body of Christ. We judge when the Scripture tells us not to. The reality of judging too quickly, not knowing, and depending on emotions keep us uninformed, immature, and judgmental becomes our normal.

The lame man's perspective tells us that this man had nothing to be excited about; begging was how he lived. This was what he did. The people were rejoicing because the power of God had changed this man.

The A/Q of every Prophet

His adaptive quality had awakened within him, and he went away praising God. This is contagious now as the people were praising God. When your life does not challenge you, rest assured that you will consistently end up in the same position.

Prophet, when you accept what God has said as beneath your privilege, you fail to exercise your A/Q or adaptive quality. The reflection of this is seen as excuses you allow to normalize in your life. With these inhibitions, you become a hindered prophet.

How many of us fail to see that we are so close to a blessing we cannot have because we will not adapt to the changes God wants in our life? Can you see yourself sitting by the gate every day? Can you see yourself begging every day?

The reality is that so many of us, as prophets in the body of Christ, become addicted to a standard beneath what God has promised, and we never understand the need to develop an adaptive quality to attain God's standards.

How many of us have been through the almost stage? I almost got my blessing. I almost got delivered. I almost got saved. I almost got The Holy Ghost. I almost saw the power of God. I almost felt God move. This man almost went into the city, but he did not because he was lame.

The buffet of excuses we repeatedly use to support our "almost stage" are the anchors of our lives that keep us from adapting and moving forth in life. We would rather use a tired, worn-out excuse and not move forth rather than allow the anointing to change us because we could adapt to understanding that God's plan works.

What does an adaptive quality do in your life? It gives you access to something you have never had access to before. So many times in life, we become frustrated as we see others blessed and we are not. We see others do things we know we should be doing, look at them, and compare ourselves. Funny how we can see these things in our self-reflections.

It is a small wonder almost every prophet, every Seer, is dealing with something today. Some are angry, some have been abandoned spiritually, some want to do their own thing as they claim they need special freedom to develop. If you're reading this, trust me; you are dealing with something; some of you are just managing it better.

The cold reality of being adaptive is different for each of us, as we see a different reflection of ourselves. Therefore, you see a different level of integrity, different types of character, and different levels of understanding. The adaptive quality differs as much as the prophets striving to become what the promises of God say about us.

The lack of a developed A/Q or adaptive quality will make you think you are cursed. Your life is the same way all the time. Then you start to think that maybe the blessings of God are not for you! Maybe I should not be blessed; maybe the blessings are not for my family or me. Maybe I will never walk into God's plan for my life.

Now you have developed the "maybe not" syndrome. What you were hoping for, you now say maybe not. Maybe not to ministry, maybe not to being a prophet, maybe not to being what God has called me to be because I'm like the man at the gate. I have nothing, and doing nothing is normal for me.

The prophet now simply uses excuses to comfort their inability to grow. The excuses bring comfort to your hurt. You have seen God bless others, and even when they come in your presence, you have rejected his leaders, who he has sent with the transfer you needed because of your issues; you did not want to allow them to help you grow and adapt.

As seers and leaders, the process of dealing with the highs and lows of life is priceless. When we like Moses, we see our reflection, choose to adapt to the situation, and grow. To handle the issues and trust God. As you do, the key to change is the adaptive quality.

You will find yourself like the man at the gate at any given time in your life; understand that you are placed in situations by God to build you and give Him the Glory.

Remember, you are his prophet, his seer, and your ability to adapt is critical to accomplish your assignment. We live in a generation that has lost faith in the prophetic gift. We must be aware of it and know how to deal with it.

CHAPTER 7

The Now Generation Lost Faith in The Prophet?

People are quick to say that something is wrong these days. Many times prophets of God are doing all they know how to do, yet still find themselves rejected.

Prophets, there are many pitfalls in this time we live. Now think about it. What has happened to you? What has happened to what was so promising for you? Prophet, you were so sure. You knew you were on your way to divine success. Suddenly, somehow people have lost faith in you, and your personal life has become a nightmare.

You look at yourself, and now your confidence is shaken. You are a body of nerves- your trust in people is extremely low as you have been hurt and wounded on the outside. Your life issues do not seem to matter because you're God's prophet; yet

The Now Generation Lost Faith in The Prophet?

you are lost in your situation. The prophet you see in the reflection of yourself is an individual who is wounded.

Guess what? Your generation has lost confidence in you, you have lost confidence in yourself, and mostly you have lost confidence in God to restore you in a situation that seems to be so unfair.

The demonic field generals of frustration and depression lead the charge against you as you minister to the nations. Your reflection is troubled, and your faith is waning. You try to be a super prophet on the outside, but your inner man is disturbed, just like Moses.

Do not forget; there is another extremely critical issue. This is the issue that you're still on the front line for God. People are coming to you for prayer. As you're ministering to them, and laying hands on them, the nightmare of your life makes you feel that you are living two separate lives.

You feel like they have lost confidence in you, and you are wondering why God is taking you through this. This may or may not be your exact story. Your story may be worse in various ways. You are in a crisis, you are in the public eye, and you cannot understand why God allows you to go through this.

Welcome to the life of a prophet when a generation you are assigned to does not believe you, and there is all hell breaking loose in your life. Jeremiah, Moses, Joseph, Daniel, Huldah, to name a few prophets, all dealt with this.

Meeting The Prophet In My Reflection

You wonder where God is, and you are facing all this, and God is still sending you forth to his people. You are doing everything you can do. You have danced, spoken in tongues, worshipped, given, and life is still in a crisis on public display.

You ask God why? You have a personal struggle, and it does not seem like his response is not adequate. Mark 9:9-30 opens us up to such a dilemma. Imagine Peter, James, and John as they, chosen Apostles, have been on the mountain with Jesus. The mountain of Transfiguration as it became known.

They have seen the glory in ways no others have ever seen. They are full of the experience, and yet they run into a demon when they return. Imagine that they have been to a special place of a special anointing, and now they must deal with a situation that has been put before them.

Have you ever gone to a meeting, and God moves mightily, and then at the same time, you run into some trouble that makes no sense to you, considering where you have just been in God?

Prophets think about this, in the meeting, there were souls saved, redeemed, deliverance, and then an old enemy shows back up in your life. You remember this enemy, he is called doubt or depression, or maybe it is his 1st cousin called pride or inflated self-worth.

Somehow, it is strange we do not see ourselves fully when we look at our reflection. We seem to miss this more often than not.

These are old enemies you have battled, Prophet, and now they are here, yet again. You start to wonder as there were just as many who said it was not God as supported you. Just as many who doubted you and the power of God. You saw and experienced God's move, and now they have robbed you, yet again of the opportunity of growth in Christ.

Think about this the experience of a lifetime, the anointing is still on you, and if your Peter, James, or John, you cannot rebuke the dumb spirit out of the boy. They have come down from the mountain, full of the Glory of God upon them.

They now face an issue that makes them look ineffective. Can you imagine what is going through their minds? They are asking Jesus why they are ineffective.

There are two valuable lessons learned.
1. They know they still have more work to do to continue developing.
2. They realize they have not seen everything yet. There are two different worlds here: the Glory, and the earth reality.

We so many times confuse the realities. We feel they should work as one, and yet, we see a generation so against submitting to God. We cannot be a part of the glory until we accept the full story of Jesus and how and what he has done for us.

Meeting The Prophet In My Reflection

Along the road of life, Prophet, there is a fellow peer who discovers what you have found upon the narrow road of life. The prophet's real covenant relationships are to be cherished. We must go through it to get to it, which is relevant for our development in the prophetic gift.

Let us, on the surface, consider the way people look at us, come to us and leave us. Often, they speak about us because of the appearance of a thing on the surface. The reality is that those things may not be true.

Terms like false prophets, money-hungry, spiritual peddlers, ineffective, do not know God, are awful things said our brothers and sisters in Christ, the prophets. Have you also heard the falsehood that Apostles and prophets were only in the Old Testament days? How uninformed we choose to be in the Body of Christ.

In Mark 9:18 a man speaks to Jesus about coming to the disciples for deliverance but they were unable to help him. He lost faith in Peter, James, and John. Today we say, I went to the prophet, all he wanted to do was stare at me, and he did not have a word for me.

Then they wanted a big offering? How many times have we heard that? Or I did not believe what the Prophet said, and they went out telling everybody.

The Now Generation Lost Faith in The Prophet?

What happens, Prophet, when in that same meeting you, yourself experienced the Glory upon your life and the haters are still hating on you. They were still calling you funny names, saying you dressed funny, criticizing you, and the Glory was upon you. Now they are sending people to you to see what you will say to them so they will have more fuel to speak against you.

The issue is they don't believe, and they need more fuel for the fire of their unbelief. They will always seek to feel good about themselves, and if you are weak, they will wreck your mentality. They attempt to smother your gift. They secretly covet your gift and mock you. Their success ultimately will ignite the spark of unhealed issues of your life, like your unsettled problems.

OK prophet, what do you do when this happens? All you know is that you have done your best. Prophets, what do we do when this happens? Everyone is looking at the prophetic gifts, and everyone is a huge critic of the mouthpiece of God. The reality of the picture you see in the reflection of yourself is based on how they see you or how you see yourself.

There is much to consider but let us look at this father, who brought his child to Jesus for healing. He describes his situation to Jesus. This man was frustrated and irritated. He had been before the front-line men of Jesus in his day, and nothing had happened. Jesus is presented with this and asks him a simple question. Jesus makes a point to ask the question. How long has the child been like this?

Meeting The Prophet In My Reflection

What you must understand is that the people of that day also talk. Imagine the discussion about who the disciples were supposed to be. Just like today, people will talk no matter how much you encourage them to be quiet to things they know little or nothing of. This was not about them on the mountain; this is about who the people felt they were and the missing element of little or no faith (Mark 9). Also, notice that the condition of the child affected those who are close to him.

Now the family is frustrated, as you can imagine, and wondering why there seems to be no help for them. Yet, the question Jesus asked them is critical. Jesus does not look at the demon; he turns to the father.

The father answers since birth. Do you mean that since this child was born he was consistently tormented by demons? Nothing has been done about nothing until now because it is only now at a crisis stage for the family. Why did they wait to bring him before Jesus?

So many times, we wait until crisis time, and we want miraculous results, and we do not have the faith to experience it. In Mark 9:19 we see Jesus', answer to him, "and saith, O faithless generation, how long shall I be with you? How long shall I suffer you? Bring him unto me." Imagine the demon who now is tearing the clothes of the child in the presence of Jesus.

The Now Generation Lost Faith in The Prophet?

Jesus is asking the father, how long have you chosen to live like this? It is important to notice that Jesus is more interested in the father at this point.

In order to fix the son with his dumb spirit, we need to consider his father and what has been allowed to prosper in the lives of his family. Remember and consider this is a generational issue. Have we taught our kids or grandkids what we have allowed so that we could get along? Consider the behavior of some of our children, and it is never an issue until it is a crisis stage.

We often see a generation of people who come to the prophet for relief, and the issue is that they do not believe. They come with an attitude that if you are supposed to be a prophet, this must happen this way. They have no faith; they depend on relying on your name as a prophet.

Things did not go the way they wanted them to go; they blame the prophet. They fan the fires of doubt and disbelief. They cause people to adopt attitudes about a gift so many do not understand. Why do we live in a generation of people who won't do the essential work needed? Will you come and expect a miracle when your faith is not operating at a miracle level?

So when your friends who you have gossiped with now need to seek God through the prophetic gift, cannot truly walk in faith because they have listened to gossip, and they have absorbed doubt and unbelief. Now, they like the child's father, now call it belief and stand in need of a miracle.

Meeting The Prophet In My Reflection

Welcome to the current generation of prophets, Monday you are sent from God. People can love you on Monday, and on Wednesday, you are not of God.

Like the father, we are a generation who wants no responsibility; we want to pay no price for the oil we seek in our lives. We will never understand that the anointing costs a great price that so many of us are unwilling to pay.

The father of this child represents both sides of the equation. There is a side of a generation of little or no faith, and there is a generation of prophets who are wounded, and God has you in the battle to show you that he is your healer and deliverer and presents Himself to the world. Remember Moses, how they saw him after he killed the Egyptian? Guess what? This is the reflection they see in you and I.

We are not just a generation that has lost faith in the Prophet; we have lost faith in God but be encouraged, Prophets. We have work to do on this issue. We must now explore our responsibility with our perceptions in our ministering to these very people.

CHAPTER 8

The Communication of The Prophets Perception

WE HAVE JUST TALKED about why this generation has lost faith in the prophet. We can do much to improve our standards and our status. We owe God this sacrifice. We are looking at our reflections, so let us look at the perception we may take on.

In the Life of a Prophet, the reception of data in the form of the senses is communication. Perception is necessary for communication because of the way a prophet discerns what is spoken. Prophets can perceive in different ways, so the responsibility of communication for a prophet involves a perception that must be born of a need.

Many times, people do not believe the prophet. There are two things to consider:

1. Is the prophet speaking out of the will of God? When a prophet speaks out of the will of God, there is no perception.

The utterance is heard, but it does not have a communicated perception that is clear and to the point.

2. Do they have or is there a real need in that person's life? There is no need, there is no perception for them to receive, and they will not believe.

The critical point here is that God moves when there is a need. We, as the prophetic community of today, need to understand Matthew 5:6. This Scripture is a personal development rallying cry for the prophet. We are assigned as prophets to hunger and thirst after righteousness. We need it. The promise of God is we are to be filled with what God has and desires to give us for servitude.

God sends his solution when there is a need. God creates conditions in our lives so that we will be able to understand the communicated perception that the prophet brings to the individual, group, or nation.

God allows things to happen (Romans 8:28) to create the need for his gifts like the prophetic to flourish. Should there be no need, there would be absolutely no understanding and no wisdom to share.

We need to see and understand that every situation has been created for an opportunity to grow and experience God. We all need to be open to what God shows us that we have not experienced. This is the process of maturing in the faith. Do we realize that we now handle things that years ago we could tolerate?

The Communication of The Prophets Perception

There is an enemy of the prophet we frequently demonstrate while moving in immaturity, called pride. This will keep us as prophets undeveloped and not able to communicate with accurate perception. We may not realize it, but we need to consider that our pride frequently turns people off.

God is concerned about the very appearance of pride. To demonstrate this point, when our perception or way of looking at something is different from how God looks at it, we are moving in our intellect and not God's. Pride smothers any need. Pride makes you depend on yourself, the Prophet, and not God.

There is no wonder that we see some prophets grow because they understand that they are anointed but know they need to be still accountable and still need to learn, even though they may have had success. God can be found where there is a need; this is where there is a birthing ability to communicate his will.

We need to realize it is not feasible to be in a world outside of Heaven, where there is no need. God has created a world for us to live in and experience needs. Our society has needs; our communities have needs; our churches, ministries, and families have needs. There is an unlimited amount of need, and this affects all of us.

The ability of any prophet to communicate accurately is dependent on the needs of that prophet. Look throughout Scripture and see that any prophet that God sent to his people had some deficiency. The prophet depended on God to meet the need. The need was what was vital. This is the type of prophet that God sends to the nations.

Think about it: the prophet now has a communication perspective on who they are and what they are sent to do. There is a marked difference between prophets, who have been through this process, versus those who have not.

We can rest assured that God will fill us with the deposited experiences, including how the world treats us and how we view our reflections. We need it all to position us to communicate with a perception that is the viewpoint of God and God alone. Welcome to what we commonly call processing. So many prophets want to avoid processing.

Whatever God forms, whatever God gifts, he supplies the gifts and allows us to see a need to develop them. Ezekiel 37 is the classic story of the dry bones. The prophet Ezekiel is set in the valley of the dry bones. Ezekiel is asked, by God, can these bones live?

The Prophet Ezekiel is put in a situation that requires him to communicate to God with God's perspective on what he has asked. He tells God from a perspective that shows that he is looking at the situation like God is. We see the miracle of life happen right before Ezekiel simply because Ezekiel has gained the ability to communicate a perspective to God that lines up with the Word of God.

The Communication of The Prophets Perception

When a prophet begins to understand how to communicate with God, that prophet will then understand how to minister to people of all cultures, races, backgrounds. Understand that respect is earned, and sharing God's perspective will bring you respect.

The key to moving forth in the prophetic is a need to understand that my perspective must be like the perspective of God. Should I ever want God to be with me, then I should know that I will have no problem doing his will if I communicate his perspective.

The flip side to this is that when you and I communicate to people with what thus saith the Lord, we have no reason to doubt or even feel we need to hang around and see what God does. We are called to do our job.

The perception you have is priceless; it is undeniable even if some will disagree with it. That is not your issue because you have learned how to communicate the perspective of God.

Do you remember the hymn the saints of the past generations used to sing? There was a song called I need thee; I need Thee every hour, yes Lord, I need thee. The ability to need God cannot be overstated in the life of a prophet.

In 2 Kings 4, The widow with the small jar of olive oil, comes to Elisha and tells her plight. The word that Elisha communicated to her through his perception that if she followed the plan, she would be fine.

Meeting The Prophet In My Reflection

There is no way she could have looked at what the Prophet said, and it made sense to her naturally. There's conviction in the prophet's words that made her look beyond what she saw when he communicated to her. Elisha had no concern of doubters and, of course, those who laughed behind the widow's back.

There is an assurance when the prophet can communicate with a perception that builds faith. Who do you know who will walk up and down the streets of their community and borrow pots? Can you see yourself in a similar situation in your life reflections?

Who do you know? Who is going to believe the word that has been given? The prophet who will do this is a believer who is walking in a level of faith beyond the shadow levels that we may be witness to in this day and time.

This is also a person who has a need to be met. Notice that the woman and her needs were walking as one. And as great as her faith was, she still needs a word that could stir her faith to another level.

She was ready because she had a need. A Prophet met the need. Elisha has a word that communicated God's perspective. This was the assurance that everything would be fine, despite what she was seeing or experiencing.

Matthew 5:6 is our development cry for the prophet. We are assigned as prophets to hunger and thirst after righteousness.

The Communication of The Prophets Perception

The promise of God is we shall be filled with what God has and desires to give us for servitude.

The ability to communicate the perspective of God is clear and not impacted by anyone or anything. The price of this is priceless in the life of a prophet.

We can find ways to blame the world and other factors on our performance. The prophet's perspective needs to line up with God's perspective. Have you considered this in your self-reflections? We must grow, and we must also realize that we are a generation blessed and weak at the same time?

CHAPTER 9

The Prophet, Generationally Blessed and Weak at the Same Time

AS PROPHETS, WE SHOULD never be jealous of each other's gifts; we should know that we are blessed for the benefit of others. This is about us as we look at our reflection. And by now, as you have read this book, you should have an idea of who you are.

One thing we all must realize is that prophets suffer for the anointing in their lives. The anointing on the prophet's life is for the generations the prophet is called to and connected to by the prophet's mantle. There are things in your life, the reflection of yourself reveals. Knowing who you are is priceless as we explore generational traits, primarily among prophets.

The enemy knows that if you ever learn how to reproduce after your kind, your spiritual sons and daughters, biological sons and daughters will not have to go through what you went through. Therefore, it is a fact; the enemy wants to kill the 5-fold ministry gifts, especially the prophet. To some of us, this is old news; to others, it is an eye-opener.

Like Moses, you will see yourself in sometimes confusing situations, and one of the most important things you can realize is that you are not perfect. The reality is that we see in the life of prophets is that we are blessed and still have faults. We are spiritual beings with human flaws.

We encourage others, and we are sometimes discouraged. We have a word for others but no word for us. Our faults are many; as prophets, sometimes we live in the facade of the outside or the surface look. While others of us live a nightmare in our private lives.

Two classic examples of this are Abraham and Isaacs, anointed, gifted, and both were liars. Both lied; what is more amazing is that we see Isaac tell the same lie that Abraham did in the previous generation, yes, the same lie. The reality is he was not born when his father told the lie that he spoke. Just like the great Moses, oh how we carry the reflections of ancestors with us.

In Genesis 20:2-7, we see that Abraham introduced his wife, Sarah, by saying, "She is my sister." King Abimelech sent for Sarah and had her brought to him at his palace.

Meeting The Prophet In My Reflection

God tells Abimelech that Abraham has lied to him, noticing that God still claimed him as his prophet. Here we see the regard God has for his prophets, and the fault of Abraham is clearly on display.

Remember this when you see yourself, and you realize you are not perfect. I'm talking about an honest self-reflection of yourself, Prophet.

Sarah was Abraham's half-sister; Abraham had told a half-truth. But a half-truth is still a lie. Genesis 20:11 (b)-12 Abraham justifies that; they will want my wife and kill me to get her.' And she is my sister, for we both have the same father, but different mothers, and I married her.

In Exodus 20:16, we see wisdom on a false witness, who has information with the wrong implication. It's saying the right thing but using it in the wrong way. Abraham gave the correct information; he gave it the wrong significance because he failed to tell Abimelech that she was his wife.

In Genesis 26:7-11, the same old sin of deception raises its ugly head again. If nothing else proves it, this does; Isaac is the son of his father. Frightened, we see Isaac succumbs to the temptation, and now he claims his wife is his sister. He risked Rebekah's purity as the price for his protection.

The deception was apparent and generational. The sin of Isaac and that of his father Abraham are so alike. Both sinned

The Prophet, Generationally Blessed and Weak at the Same Time

in the presence of Abimelech, and the ruler of the Philistines rebuked both.

Both had beautiful wives, and both feared for their safety. Both lied, and it seems that Abraham nor Isaac recognized the gravity of their sin or fully repented.

Look at the sin. This is a cycle. This is a pattern, a curse of doomed activity. Yet today, I mention this to you because some of you look at yourselves and see ways you do not want to leave.

Patterns, or cycles we accept, and then we complain about why God will not take this away. Could it be that we will not allow him?

This is present today, a cycle of behavior where a leader's spirit is both generationally blessed and weak at the same time. The inherited generation, that's us, the current generation, who inherited this from Abraham just as his son did. The question is, how does Isaac break the curse of Abraham? How do we break the dysfunctional cycle in our lives?

Isaac sowed a seed amid trouble in his life. Today many prophets will benefit from this. Unfortunately, many will not do this because of ideas and concepts of seed sowing. Sow a seed amid the issues in your life; Isaac did just that. He knew his father was blessed despite his shortcomings in his marriage, his mentality, and his ministry. What does he know that we do not?

Meeting The Prophet In My Reflection

Look at Genesis 8:22. The only way to change a cycle and break a curse is with a seed. This is a seedtime and harvest world. You break the cycle and stop the cycle with a seed. Genesis 26:12-25, in verse 2, God promised to guide Isaac to where he would live his life. God leads Isaac back to His promise to Abraham. God uses adversity and opposition to bless us and mature us.

So many prophets in their service for the Lord are thinking, "God can't use me. God would not use me. God won't use me because I've failed so miserably; I've messed up so badly." That's the voice of the enemy.

God is our source, and we will have to deal with the demons of yesteryear because God wants to give some prophets a move forward anointing.

So many Prophetic and gifted people of God find themselves trapped in the attributes of yesterday. We see them within us and know they are still holding us back. We must break the strongholds.

Read and reread Leviticus 26:40-46 and Hosea 4:6. I have not quoted either Scripture, so please take a moment to read them both to understand the importance.

We see our reflections, and we are another generation doing the same thing that the previous generation does. Why does this happen? Why do prophets duplicate the same activity, same weakness? We see the cycles of behavior.

The Prophet, Generationally Blessed and Weak at the Same Time

This is present today, a cycle of behavior where when the spirit of a leader is caught, we see the same attributes in the spiritual or biological son or daughter. Why does this happen?

Why do prophets duplicate the same activity, same weakness? We see the cycles of behavior. Deuteronomy 5:9 tells us that the sins of the father are passed down.

As you look at yourself, let's now interject here so that you will know four essential things:

- The first important nugget you need to know is where your Gilgal is located. This is the place of faith. You must learn how to live by faith and trust God.

- The second thing you need to know is where your Bethel is located. The place of commitment and decision. This is the place of no turning back and death to the old man in our life.

- The third thing you need to know is where your Jericho is located. This is the place of warfare, the place where you inherit the enemy of your father, biological or spiritual. This is Isaac and Abraham. Sooner or later, the same enemy will come against you. This is a cycle.

Look at David: he is known for his sexual appetite. Can you say, Bathsheba? David had a son named Amnon, who raped

Meeting The Prophet In My Reflection

his sister Tamar; he has another son named Solomon, who had thousands of concubines.

This was his daddy's devil. Understand that you are going to fight your daddy's devil. You will deal with it. The sins of the father are passed to the son.

*The fourth thing you need to know is where your Jordan is located. This is the place where you will learn how to see. You begin to see. This also is the output of the birthing from your prophetic lineage.

Prophets, we are like Isaac, son of Abraham. Many of us today deal with the devil of our forefathers, both spiritual and biological. We are the inherited generation.

Abraham's policy of deception was a policy established before he entered any danger. This is the work of fear, and see how it was passed along to his son. We may think we will not have to admit it in our own lives, but we will.

God is our source, and we will have to deal with the demons of yesteryear because God wants to give some prophets a right now blessing! God sees you on a whole new level. Did you realize that? Look at yourself again and shout Glory!

CHAPTER 10

How God Sees the Prophet on Another Level

We have been discussing your reflection along with the reflection of Moses. Go back and reread about the four winds if you are still unsure about the type of prophet you align with.

Look at your self-reflection again. What does it show you about yourself? Now, what do you choose to do about the issues of your life? Can you handle the fact that despite you, God sees you on another level?

Today's prophet must be connected in the culture to make a difference. They must be grounded to serve the assigned people of your life. Our God is famous for using ordinary people to do extraordinary things.

One such relationship that reflects this is in the person of Peter, a man who was assigned and connected to his culture.

Meeting The Prophet In My Reflection

He was a Biblical reality figure. As we look at his life, we see and get an abundance of lessons for today's Prophet, to never be discouraged.

As Peter matured as a man and as a gift of God, he set an example of how God can see us on one level, and yet, we fail to act on the promises of God. The reality is that, like many of us, Peter never knew who he was. Like many prophets who aspire to be prophets, and effective Seers for God, so many times we are like Peter.

We have no reference point on how to start, no reference on how to do it and no reference on who to do it with. This was Peter when he met Jesus, and this is us today as we are looking to start somewhere.

When Peter met Jesus, he was a fisherman; while there is nothing wrong with being a fisherman, Jesus saw him as a fisher of men. The reality was that Jesus saw a calling upon his life that would allow him to operate on a higher level than he was operating.

Notice what Jesus said in Matthew 4:18-19. 18 Jesus saw Simon called Peter, and Andrew his brother. He saw them cast a net into the sea. They were fishermen. There is nothing wrong with being a fisherman. Jesus saw them on another level.

The reality is that Peter is unfamiliar with what Jesus sees. Do you see that Peter was doing what he was doing on a different type of level than Jesus saw him? Jesus now sees and offers to take him on to a higher level.

Look at you, your ability to pray, speak for God, and you know the Word of God. Still, there is something that somehow you see in your life as a multitude of drama, situations and it seems like one disaster after the other. You feel you are not going anywhere.

The life lessons from your life history give you a snapshot of your destiny's specific aspects. Think back on your life, Prophets, and see how you are uniquely prepared for your calling now and where God is taking you.

I'm talking about how God sees you on your current level and on your next level. Your life issues are the moments of training, moments of experience, and the moments of finding out that you can trust God, and the time you find out that God is for you and has called you to another level amid the drama of your life. Welcome to the uneven aspect of growth.

Have you noticed that when God uses you to help people, it is often based on your history? Where you were, has uniquely trained you for the level you are at now, to do the work of God and to be effective doing it. Thank God for what you have been through. It paved the road for where you are now.

Let's look now at Luke 5, the initial phase of the mentality of Peter as he goes to another level. Here we see his mentality. Jesus uses his boat to teach, and he wants to bless him. We see

Meeting The Prophet In My Reflection

after Jesus speaks; he says to Peter to launch out into the deep. "Master, we have toiled all night", says Peter., but at your word. So, when his boat did, they encountered so many fish, their nets broke.

Imagine all the boats now filled with fish, and now Peter falls at his knees and tells Jesus he is not worthy and please depart from him. This is the struggle of going to another level. This is the struggle many have today and how they see themselves once they feel their reflection has been exposed with their faults.

Peter is worshiping, yet he proclaims that he is not worthy of the blessing nor worthy of a lofty calling. This is the struggle of the Prophet moving forth. Peter has no faith that Jesus is in his life to bless him and prosper him. By his own words, we see that Peter does not yet believe. The mentality must be in perspective to the level of faith you will operate in.

Prophet, until your faith shows up in your personal life, it will not show up in your ministry. Until your faith shows up in your ministry, Prophet, you will not show up to demonstrate who God has called you to be.

Prophet, if your faith has not shown up, you have not developed the temperament to see obstacles and know that they are not permanent in your life. This is real talk and necessary for prophetic growth. Look at your reflection of yourself again and apply this. You have read this book so far; make sure you understand that your faith is necessary for prophetic growth.

How God Sees the Prophet on Another Level

The lack of faith demonstrates its needs; unbelief manifests in several forms, from spiritual to physical. Have you ever seen a prophet with no stamina to do anything for God? They want the title; they master the excuses and want to be left alone, even when you do see more for them.

Then there is the Peter-type prophet called, but you do not believe that you are called. Your calling shows you that the level you will eventually work on is more significant than your current level.

Do you remember when you were going around fishing within the body of Christ to see who would call or recognize you as a prophet? This happens because of being unsure and not trusting or being able to process the issues of your life.

You do not understand where you are, yet God is sending people to tell you that you are more than you realize. Learn how to see people; they may be more than you think. They may have come to prosper you, and you are rejecting them because your faith has not shown up.

This was the issue for Peter. Peter needed faith, and his confidence has not shown up in the vision of what he is bound to become as of this time in his life. Peter let's Jesus, who to him was a stranger, use his boat. His life changed on that day.

It was evident that Peter had heard of Jesus. Peter demonstrates Matthew 17:20, "And Jesus said unto them, Because of your unbelief: for verily I say unto you, If ye have faith as a grain of mustard seed, ye shall say unto this mountain, remove hence to yonder place, and it shall remove, and nothing shall be impossible unto you."

This is the mind of Peter; in the realm of faith, he is operating as having faith as less than a grain of a mustard seed. Despite his apparent lack of faith, he is still positioned for God. He is seen as a critical player in the movement.

How many times do we see ourselves like Peter? We are positioned, but because we do not witness the glamor, the splendor, or the recognition, we do not feel like God has placed us. We cannot see, and yet the place God puts you or the place God does not put you reflects greatly on your assignment.

Those of you who remember after the boat incident, there was a closeness between Peter and Jesus. What kind of miracle has God had to perform to get your attention to spur a relationship with you. Peter saw how he launched out into the deep and what would happen when he trusted the word of the Lord.

Now the relationship is established, and we see Peter's character revealed, and the process starts. Look closer at the character of Peter.

He is a conflicted individual like many of today's now-generation Prophets. He is new to building relationships, and the initial conflict we see is when Jesus tells him to follow him.

How God Sees the Prophet on Another Level

This means Peter must walk away from a world of fishing; all he has known is to work in a world of fishing for human beings. In other words, he must make the changes. The changes the relationship brings challenge Peter to his very core to change.

Prophet, you may be called, but you must realize that part of that calling is that you must walk away from something to realize how God sees you in his plan for your life. For Peter, it was fishing, and yet fishing was the very thing that positioned him for greatness.

As we look at Peter, like most prophets, the hardest thing in the world is to walk away from what you had made up in your mind to do. Think about it, when we make up our minds to do something so many times, not even God can change our minds. Our nature is one of being stubborn, bullheaded, and peculiar because of our uncontrolled emotions.

The beautiful thing is that Peter has changed his mind and decided to follow Jesus. The way Jesus sees Peter is he is one to be a proponent of miracles, and yet the opportunity Jesus affords him is one of the uncommon miracles.

Who remembers Peter walking on water and learning the lesson of how to focus and why it is essential? Later, Peter matured to be so anointed that he leads the early church as his shadow is the healing element for literally thousands of people.

Meeting The Prophet In My Reflection

Do you think that Peter saw himself doing what he was doing for God? The reality is that Jesus saw him with all his faults on another level than where he was at.

A relationship with God is critical to the Prophet's gifts. Have you ever noticed that the enemy of God wants to isolate you and keep you from the people who have your transfer? The perks of the Prophetic ministry are in the relationships we have with God and each other.

Relationships open portals: the right relationships open us to sights unseen and opportunities galore. Peter would have never been the Peter we see develop into a man of faith and Power unless he had the right relationships in his life. There is an old saying. You are "next," as in your connections. Who have you connected to that values the relationship? The key here is the value of the relationship.

Connect with people who can see you doing it. Connect with people who can see you being. Connect with people who understand honor, respect, and integrity, and you will connect with people who will see you on another level. One final thought is you, as a prophet, must place value in your relationships.

Do you remember Peter who denied Jesus? After what he said in Matthew 26:33, "I will not deny you, I will die if I have to, but I will not deny you. We all know how that went. "Like many of us today, Peter, when the pressure is on us, we tend to fold and throw in the towel. The pressure was on as Jesus was hanging on the cross, and now there are questions about his followers. Peter denies him despite his boast.

Understand that Peter is still a work in progress like us today. This is the same Peter who was on the mountain of transfiguration, the same Peter who walked with Jesus, the same Peter who walked on water, the same Peter who cut a soldier's ear off when they came to get Jesus, and now he is still a work in progress.

Do you find it funny to see the know-it-all Apostle or the know everything Prophet who brags and boasts about their years of godly service? When the pressure is on, they disappear. We need direction; they are lost. We all know them, or maybe we are them today.

Peter's mistake was he did not acknowledge Jesus when the heat was on when Jesus was crucified. There is still growth to be realized in Peter. To deny a relationship is a definition of the value of the relationship. Luke 9:26, "Who is ashamed of the anointed one and his anointing?" Relationships in the life of a prophet are critical. Examine your inner circle and see who sees you for being more than you may be now.

Now look at your circles connected to your life and see who sees you on another level. Who sees you as an Apostle, a Prophet, A Seer, a Watchman, who looks at you and sees greatness and is willing to stand with you through the process of becoming?

Jesus stood with Peter through his process, just like a mentor will stand with a mentee through their process. The relationship is one of a spiritual intimacy that reveals the flaws we see in the life of who many referred to as cussing Peter. Speaking of spiritual intimacy, let us explore its reflection in the John the Baptist Anointing.

CHAPTER 11

Prophets Moving in The John the Baptist Anointing

MOST PROPHETS KNOW THAT the anointing is the yoke destroying and burden removing power of God. We see this very fact spoken to us in Scripture at Isaiah 10:27. Do we see this in our reflections is the question I ask. In the last few chapters, our focus has been getting an understanding of ourselves better. We need to see the whole picture of ourselves in our reflections.

I want to discuss a unique prophet of God, a man known as John the Baptist. Like David, John the Baptist does not get enough credit for his ministry and his work. John the Baptist discovered some convenient and valuable tips as John the Baptist developed in his anointing.

Let us look at the prophetic lessons involving John the Baptist and his life. He is sent to prepare the people for Jesus. Imag-

Meeting The Prophet In My Reflection

ine the life of Jesus from birth, and now around the age of 30, we see his ministry started.

He is eligible for the priesthood, and Jesus goes from isolation to being celebrated. The fact that Jesus did not begin his ministry until he was 30 is not a reflection of the picture many prophets would want to deal with.

The first issue you must learn is that Jesus goes from isolation to being celebrated. Every prophet who refuses to go through this process will forfeit their ministry. There will be seasons and years that you will be an unnamed ministry.

This is complicated and seemingly unfair for prophets and seers in their development in their self-evaluations of themselves. Your self-evaluation should line up with God's objectives. You have no objectives when you are submitted to God other than to please him.

The saga of witnessing the work of prophets and Seers as they attempt to duck this step is discouraging. Everybody wants to be somebody, and the fact that God does this his way makes prophets many times jump before it's their time. Look at our role model in John the Baptist.

Imagine that no one will know you, no one will celebrate you, and yet this is the time for you to develop. Then imagine that people do know you as an outsider. You do not fit in. Peers of John the Baptist felt he was insignificant. Others knew he dared to be different.

Can we say this about you as we look at your reflection of how you see yourself? All these things could have been said about John the Baptist, but God was with him in his assignment.

Prophets, you must know that you are still a work in progress. Maybe you are not accustomed to being out front, nor have you developed the skills for such an assignment that you seek.

The issue of strengthening your relationship with God seems to be secondary to many because your eyes are on the wrong focus. The John the Baptist gift will keep you focused.

Prophets take notice of this: the needed wisdom, character, and mentality for your assignments must be developed with the required tools of your craft within the relationship you build with God. Look at Jesus; he demonstrates this process for at least 18 years in the life of Jesus from age 12 to 30, no one heard anything of him. Then his ministry started.

In John 1:29 -36, the Bible reveals the picture of John the Baptist baptizing people in the Jordan river. While baptizing, John declared, "behold the lamb of God." This is the announcement of Jesus to the world. Why is this significant to prophets? Every prophet, and every seer needs a John the Baptist prophetic figure in your life.

You need someone who God anoints to announce you to the world. Look around us, look in our prophetic community and investigate the body of Christ; we have far too many self-appointed and self-announced gifts. God is a God that can bring you to the celebration stage of ministry.

He is able, and the reality is that God does not need our help. He has a John the Baptist who he has assigned to your life, who will and can announce you to your community, your peers, and your country when needed.

Prophets, it is not your ego, or your family affiliations, it is God using a John the Baptist in your life for his purposes. The purposes of God. He has the plan, and your agenda is irrelevant. In moments we see Jesus go from being simply a person in the crowd to someone everybody knew.

This happened in moments. When this happens in your life as God elevates you, will you know how to handle the newfound celebration of your ministry? You will not unless you are prepared.

Let us not kid ourselves; we all know of a situation that we have seen or experienced in ministry where there was an absence of a John the Baptist or an individual rebuked their John the Baptist. Often, they then feel like they were celebrated but found out they were only tolerated.

Every prophet needs a senior prophet to point him or her out. You need someone to call you, and present you to the world. Again, Jesus was not self-appointed, and every prophet or anyone who would aspire to be a prophet should know and recognize this fact.

Look at Luke 1:41-44 and imagine the saga of Elizabeth, mother of John the Baptist, and Mary, mother of Jesus. How ironic it was that the day that they visited together both were pregnant. There is leaping in the womb of Elizabeth, and she is filled with the Spirit of God.

John the Baptist was being anointed in the process. We are now privy to see a total turnaround as we see that John the Baptist is the one God uses to announce Jesus to the world.

The point here is that we learn that you never know who someone may be to you in the Body of Christ. Relationships are necessary and precious in the Body of Christ.

Look, we now see Jesus baptized in the Jordan River by John the Baptist. There is a unity we see symbolized with Jesus and John the Baptist. From the wombs and now to the Jordan River. Far too many prophets go out of their way to demonstrate that they need no one and do not have covenant relationships.

We also see the future symbolized as John the Baptist is different from the peers of his time. He is not the traditional servant of God of his time; he is different. One of the needed traits of today's prophets is not to be afraid to be different. When you look at your reflection and you see something different than others, that is just fine.

Meeting The Prophet In My Reflection

As a prophet/seer, you will be different. You will be the one who will stand out in the crowd and see things differently as the purposes of Jesus are fulfilled through your life.

John the Baptist was one such prophet who we see was not afraid to be different. He was different in his dress, his ministry, and he was controversial because he did not fit the status quo. Does this describe you in a few words? How do you look in your reflections?

Are you frightened at the thought of being different, or are you intimidated by controversy, or are you running from place-to-place gossiping about your prophetic peers or people because they are different from who you are?

The prophet today who God will use is radical; they are not scared. The prophet who carries the John the Baptist gift is not moved by what they see in people's eyes. They are only driven by what they believe. The more people talked about John the Baptist, the more he ministered the gospel.

Prophets who want a John the Baptist gift need to seek a John the Baptist mentality. Without the mentality, you will be ineffective with the gift, simply because you will always be looking over your shoulder or trying to understand how others feel about what God is telling you to do.

Prophets, the John the Baptist anointing does not try to impress you; it has no desire to entertain you. The only thing it wants to do is fulfill the God-given assignment, this is the gift of a worker, a servant of God, clearly focused.

John the Baptist demonstrated this with his very life. As a prophet, you will speak just as loud with your life, if not louder, than your voice. Are you focused, and are you ready for what God has given you?

The John the Baptist anointing represents a gift that is matured in its due season. The gift has been through its share of the storms of life, sickness, gossip, lies, laughter, rejection, poverty, and being outcast. This gift is willing to do whatever it takes to get the job for God done.

This gift will fight for God; it can be deployed in almost any place because it is faithful and understands that the mission of God is more important than anything else in its life.

Are you willing to walk past your peers for God? Are you ready to walk through their critiques and can you deal with the ditches they dig for you? John the Baptist demonstrated this and more with his life. You cannot have this kind of gift for a show; it is strictly for God.

When you have been through too much to return to where you used to be, you will understand that the development of this gift is precious beyond words. The anointing of John the Baptist does three things:

1. It will tell you your identity.

Meeting The Prophet In My Reflection

2. It opens you up to an anointing you have never been under.
3. It will not allow your situation to define you.

Now my prayer is that you are better equipped to see more of your reflection as you look at yourself. Look again at the reflection of that prophet in your mirror. Now go and meet God's prophet again.

Blessings and thank you, my friend.
Apostle Ken Cox

About The Author

God is expanding the work of Apostle Ken Cox as he shares on social media platforms and produces a network of Prophetic Teachings on Roku TV. Apostle Cox teaches and ministers at various types of meetings.

Apostle Cox serves the Body of Christ as a Prophet sent to the Nations. He is married to Prophetess Sabina Cox as they lead Where Eagles Fly Fellowship LLC. WEF provides empowerment to Seers globally. The website is www.whereeaglesfly.us, and you can call Apostle Cox at 919-695-3375 or email at ApostleCox@gmail.com.

Index

4

4 Winds, 10

A

A/Q, 43, 44, 45, 46, 49, 50
abandon, 31
Abimelech, 69, 70, 71
Abraham, 26, 27, 32, 33, 69, 70, 71, 72, 73, 74
accountable, 63
adaptable quality, 43, 46, 47
adversity, 4, 72
affiliations, 88
agenda, 88
Amos, 39
ancestors, 69
Andrew, 76
angel, 12
angry, 46, 50
anointed, 9, 16, 22, 63, 69, 81, 83, 89
anointing, 13, 22, 32, 37, 41, 42, 50, 54, 55, 60, 68, 72, 83, 85, 90, 91, 92

Index

Apostle, 19, 37, 44, 83, 92, 93
Apostle Paul, 19, 37
assignment, 1, 12, 21, 23, 29, 33, 51, 80, 87, 91

B

basket, 3
battle, 21, 31, 60
behavior, 59, 71, 72, 73
beneficiaries, 36, 37
benefit, 42, 68, 71
Bethel, 73
bitter, 46
blame, 25, 59, 67
blessed, 4, 5, 34, 50, 67, 68, 69, 71
blind, 31
Body of Christ, 41, 48, 56, 89, 93
bondage, 8, 22, 27
book, 1, 28, 39, 68, 78
bullheaded, 81
burdens, 15
bushfires, 35
business, 6, 44

C

captive, 31
cattle, 32
celebrate, 86
CEO, 33
challenges, 46, 47

child, 3, 14, 57, 58, 59, 60
church life, 41
clothes, 4, 58
communication, 61, 64
confrontation, 40
confusion, 5
conviction, 40, 66
correction, 17
counsel, 17, 18
covenant, 23, 38, 42, 56, 89
creator, 26
credit, 20, 85
crowd, 88, 90
crucifixion, 19
cruelness, 14
culture, 4, 75
curse, 26, 71, 72
curses, 19, 22

D

Daniel, 32, 33, 53
David, 9, 15, 19, 20, 21, 23, 73, 85
deception, 70, 74
decision, 48, 73
defeated, 39
deliverance, 18, 19, 28, 30, 31, 37, 54, 56
deliverer, 60
demonic spirits, 18, 19
demons, 19, 36, 58, 72, 74

demonstrate, 40, 63, 78, 89
depressed, 46
destiny, 14, 30, 77
destroy, 13, 23, 30
destructive, 12, 14
direction, 11, 13, 23, 83
disbelief, 59
discernment, 15
disobedience, 13, 15
displacement, 8
distractions, 30
Divine Grace, 26, 27
divine success, 52
door, 36, 37, 42
doubt, 31, 54, 59, 65
drama, 6, 44, 77
dream, 26, 32
dysfunctional, 46, 71

E

earth, 11, 18, 37, 55
East wind prophets, 11, 13
economic oppression, 32, 33
educated, 4
Egyptian, 4, 5, 6, 7, 8, 60
Elisha, 9, 65, 66
Elizabeth, 89
emotion, 8
empowerment, 24, 93

encourage, 58, 69

end-time plan, 36, 37

endure, 27

enemies, 20, 27, 55

evil, 12, 13, 15, 16, 19, 25, 36, 44

exploits, 7

expose, 15

eyes, 5, 87, 90

Ezekiel, 14, 16, 17, 64

F

fail, 15, 49, 76

faith, 15, 23, 26, 51, 52, 53, 56, 58, 59, 60, 61, 62, 66, 73, 78, 79, 80, 82

faithful, 91

false prophet, 26

false witness, 70

falsehood, 56

father, 57, 58, 59, 60, 69, 70, 71, 73, 74

faults, 69, 78, 82

fear, 7, 8, 31, 74

fearful, 30

fighting, 1, 5, 7, 48

fisher of men, 76

foods, 4

forfeit, 86

forsaken, 20

four corners, 11

four winds, 11, 35, 75

freedom, 28, 50
fruits of the Spirit, 37
frustration, 8, 53

G

garden, 28
generation, 6, 13, 16, 31, 45, 51, 53, 55, 58, 59, 60, 61, 67, 69, 71, 72, 74, 80
generational, 59, 68, 70
Gentiles, 16
gift, 1, 2, 6, 9, 14, 19, 20, 32, 51, 56, 57, 59, 76, 87, 90, 91
gifts, 8, 32, 57, 62, 64, 68, 69, 82, 88
glory, 1, 42, 54, 55
God, 1, 3, 6, 8, 9, 10, 11, 12, 13, 14, 15, 16, 17, 18, 19, 20, 21, 22, 23, 24, 25, 26, 27, 28, 29, 30, 31, 32, 33, 34, 35, 36, 37, 38, 39, 40, 41, 42, 43, 45, 47, 48, 49, 50, 51, 52, 53, 54, 55, 56, 57, 59, 60, 61, 62, 63, 64, 65, 66, 67, 70, 71, 72, 73, 74, 75, 76, 77, 78, 79, 80, 81, 82, 85, 86, 87, 88, 89, 90, 91, 92, 93
gold, 32
gossip, 23, 59, 91
grace, 31, 37, 41
grandson, 4
gravity, 71
Greek, 11
growth, 2, 31, 40, 45, 55, 77, 78, 83

H

harmful, 30

healer, 60
healing balms, 37
Heaven, 63
Hebrew, 4, 5, 6, 7, 8, 11
hell, 53
heritage, 4, 6, 7
history, 77
Holy Ghost, 49
hope, 1, 19, 29, 31
hopelessness, 8
Hosea, 13, 40, 72
Huldah, 53
humanity, 26
hurricanes, 26

I

identity, 5, 7, 45, 91
idolatry, 13
inability, 51
ineffective, 34, 55, 56, 90
inherit, 28, 40, 73
internet, 17
Isaac, 69, 70, 71, 72, 73, 74
Isaiah, 14, 16, 85
isolation, 86
Israel, 8, 13, 15, 16, 20, 22, 27, 32, 39, 40, 42

J

James, 15, 54, 55, 56
jealous, 23, 68
Jeremiah, 11, 53
Jericho, 73
Jerusalem, 16, 32
Jesus, 16, 20, 22, 54, 55, 56, 57, 58, 59, 76, 77, 78, 79, 80, 81, 82, 83, 84, 85, 86, 87, 88, 89, 90
John the Baptist, 11, 13, 84, 85, 86, 87, 88, 89, 90, 91
Jordan, 74, 87, 89
Joseph, 9, 53
Judah, 14
judge, 7, 19, 25, 48
judgement, 26

K

Ken Cox, 92, 93
keys, 1
keyword, 3, 12
king, 19, 20, 32
King, 16, 26, 32, 33, 69
King Solomon, 16

L

labor, 32
lame, 45, 46, 47, 48, 49
Laodiceans, 15
leader, 7, 8, 44, 46, 71, 73
liberation, 22

lifetime, 4, 55
locusts, 18
Lord, 16, 17, 19, 21, 22, 23, 24, 31, 65, 72, 80
love, 6, 15, 25, 60

M

magnitude, 6, 8
mantle, 9, 17, 40, 41, 42, 68
Mark, 20, 22, 54, 56, 58
Matthew, 11, 15, 20, 62, 66, 76, 79, 82
maturity, 12, 31
Mediterranean Sea, 13
mentality, 1, 8, 11, 57, 71, 77, 78, 87, 90
mercy, 41
mess, 27
message, 22, 34, 40
mimicked, 40
minister, 31, 53, 65
miracle, 59, 64, 80
miracles, 22, 23, 81
mirror, 3, 4, 9, 92
mission, 9, 10, 34, 36, 91
Monday, 60
moody, 46
Moses, 3, 4, 5, 6, 7, 8, 9, 18, 24, 39, 43, 48, 51, 53, 60, 69, 75
mountain of Transfiguration, 54
mountains, 29
Mulberry Trees, 20
mysteries, 35

Index

N

nation, 3, 39, 62
neighbors, 15
new lineage, 39
nightmare, 52, 53, 69
North wind, 18, 33, 35, 36, 37, 38, 39, 40, 41, 42

O

oath, 20
obey, 15
obstacles, 78
Old Testament, 19, 56
olive oil, 65
opinions, 17
opportunity, 4, 55, 62, 81
oppression, 26, 32, 33
outsider, 8, 39, 86
overflowing shower, 16

P

pandemic, 1
peace, 17, 33
peers, 23, 24, 32, 88, 89, 90, 91
Pentecost, 11
perception, 61, 62, 63, 64, 65, 66
personal life, 52, 78

personhood, 1
Peter, 54, 55, 56, 75, 76, 77, 78, 79, 80, 81, 82, 83, 84
Pharaoh, 4
Philistines, 20, 39, 71
pitfalls, 52
planet, 17
plans, 18, 20, 37, 45
platform, 7
poor, 15, 31
poverty, 44, 91
power, 14, 36, 48, 49, 55, 85
prayer, 26, 33, 53, 92
preach, 15
pregnant, 89
pressure, 25, 82, 83
priceless, 51, 65, 67, 68
pride, 54, 63
priesthood, 86
prince, 4, 7
principle, 41
prodigal son, 32
promise, 17, 27, 62, 67, 72
prophecies, 19
Prophetess Deborah, 21, 22
Prophetess Sabina Cox, 93
prophetic, 1, 9, 12, 13, 14, 19, 20, 23, 24, 36, 39, 40, 41, 42, 43, 45, 51, 56, 57, 59, 62, 65, 74, 78, 85, 87, 90
prophetic growth, 78
Prophetic Teachings, 93
prosperity, 32

Index

Prosperity of Grace, 36
prostitute, 40
protection, 70
provision, 36, 37
punishment, 14, 16
purity, 70
purpose, 18

R

rain, 13, 37, 38
rainstorms, 14
reality, 3, 7, 8, 16, 31, 44, 46, 48, 49, 50, 55, 56, 57, 69, 76, 82, 88
reap, 30
Rebekah, 70
recover, 28
Red Sea, 15, 18
reflection, 1, 2, 3, 4, 5, 6, 7, 9, 10, 11, 12, 13, 15, 17, 18, 20, 21, 22, 24, 25, 26, 33, 34, 35, 37, 42, 43, 44, 45, 46, 47, 49, 50, 51, 53, 55, 57, 60, 68, 70, 75, 78, 84, 86, 87, 89, 92
reflections, 3, 5, 7, 8, 9, 10, 15, 33, 50, 61, 64, 66, 67, 69, 72, 85, 90
rejected, 47, 51, 52
relationships, 6, 40, 56, 80, 82, 89
repent, 17
rescue, 28
responsibility, 60, 61
restoration, 18, 19, 22, 24, 27, 32, 36
restore, 18, 53
revelation, 1, 14, 20, 31, 41

righteousness, 36, 62, 66
river, 87
rocky cliffs, 29
Rome, 28

S

sacrifice, 19, 27, 61
sad, 46
safety, 17, 71
Samuel, 19, 20, 38, 39
Satan, 31
Saul, 20
Savior, 17
Scripture, 3, 27, 32, 48, 62, 63, 72, 85
seedtime, 72
Seer, 22, 44, 50, 83
servant, 16, 89, 91
shaken, 52
shame, 40
sickness, 44, 91
silver, 32
Simon, 76
sister, 69, 70, 74
slander, 23
smartphones, 17
South wind, 24, 25, 26, 27, 28, 29, 30, 31, 32, 33, 34, 36, 41
Southern Hemisphere, 35
Sow, 30, 71
Spices, 37

spirit, 11, 15, 20, 28, 55, 59, 71, 73
spiritual dangers, 17
spiritual intimacy, 84
spiritual sons, 68
splendor, 80
stamina, 79
status quo, 38, 90
stomachs, 16
stormy wind, 16
stranger, 79
strategies, 18
stubborn, 81
suffered, 1
sustaining, 40
sweet-smelling fragrances, 37
syndrome, 51

T

technology, 4
temptation, 29, 30, 36, 70
Ten Commandments, 39
throne, 4, 36
tongue, 19
torment, 7
Tornadoes, 26
tropical storms, 26
trouble, 5, 6, 15, 43, 54, 71
trust, 29, 30, 45, 50, 51, 52, 73, 77
truth, 6, 16, 28, 44, 70

U

unbelief, 18, 22, 57, 59, 79, 80
utterance, 62

V

vain, 15, 16
victorious, 20
visions, 13, 14, 16
visitation, 42
voice, 17, 21, 39, 72, 91
voices, 17

W

war, 20, 22, 24
warrior, 19
Watchman, 17, 83
water, 13, 81, 83
weak, 57, 67, 71
Wednesday, 60
West wind, 17, 18, 19, 20, 21, 22, 23, 24, 28, 36, 41
wife, 21, 26, 32, 69, 70
wind of restoration, 18
wisdom, 18, 31, 62, 70, 87
wishy-washy, 46
woman, 4, 66
Word of God, 64, 77

world, 15, 25, 31, 60, 63, 64, 67, 72, 81, 87, 88, 89
worthy, 16, 78
writings, 19
wrong attitude, 30

Z

zeal, 1, 47

www.ingramcontent.com/pod-product-compliance
Lightning Source LLC
Chambersburg PA
CBHW052109110526
44592CB00013B/1533